Bruno Nardini

MICHELANGELO

Biography of a Genius

Original title: *Incontro con Michelangiolo*
Translation: Catherine Frost

www. giunti.it

© 1999 Giunti Editore S.p.A.
Via Bolognese 165 - 50139 Florence - Italy
Via Dante 4 - 20121 Milan - Italy

Reprint				Year		
12	11	10	9	2011	2010	2009

Printed by Giunti Industrie Grafiche S.p.A. – Prato (Italy)

PART ONE

In the workshop of the living,
at the school of the dead

NEAR THE END of the Fifteenth Century Florence was a great construction site. Filippo Strozzi had recruited an army of builders for his palace right in the heart of the city. The streets were blocked by the rubble of demolished houses. Caravans of carts, mules and donkeys raised clouds of dust as they plied their way between city and countryside.

The Gondi family was building, the friars of Santo Spirito and those of Sant'Agostino were building. They were building in Borgo Pinti, in Cestello, in the Sant'Ambrogio quarter. Lorenzo de' Medici, after having finished the pavilions in the garden of San Marco, was having the Cascine landscaped and the foundations laid for a palace at Poggio a Caiano. The workers of the Opera del Duomo were completing the lantern atop the dome of Santa Maria del Fiore.

Within the third circle of its walls, which still enclosed orchards and gardens, Florence was changing overnight. Inspired by the example of the rich, the common people too had been infected by the «building disease», and the government of the Signoria, fanning the flames, was granting forty years of exemption from taxes to anyone who decided to erect a new construction.

There was work for all. «The men of that time», reported the chroniclers, «were so caught up in the frenzy to build, that there was not one builder left free in Florence».

In the streets of Florence one might meet Michelozzo and Giuliano da Sangallo, Verrocchio and Sandro Botticelli, the young Leonardo da Vinci and the gentle Lorenzo di Credi, the youthful Machiavelli, still in search of a position, and the scholarly Poliziano leaving the palace in Via Larga in the company of Count Pico della Mirandola.

In the climate of that great renovation the best lesson, for any art or trade, was taught by example. Every artist had his pupils, every master his shop boy. From the workshop of Donatello had come architects like Michelozzo and sculptors like Bertoldo; from that of Verrocchio had emerged Botticelli, Perugino, Lorenzo di Credi and Leonardo. In the workshop of Ghirlandaio, commissioned by Giovanni Tornabuoni to fresco the choir of Santa Maria Novella, were his brothers David and Benedetto as well as a group of promising young men: Giuliano Bugiardini and Francesco Granacci, Jacopo known as Indaco and the boy Michelangelo Buonarroti.

But the lessons taught by the living were not enough. Grinding powers and mixing colors for a fresco, transferring a drawing from cartoon to plastered wall or highlighting a figure were good experience, but not enough in themselves. On the contrary, they were the stimulus for a new, more direct approach. And so the boys met in groups, going to look at Giotto in Santa Croce, or Masaccio in the Carmine, or the Beato Angelico in San Marco. Here, free from the demands of their masters, they could study genius at first hand.

«So we're all agreed. Tomorrow it's Giotto, in Santa Croce!».

That band of shabbily dressed boys met at the appointed hour in the Peruzzi Chapel. Sprawling on the floor, leaning against the altar, standing on a bench, they copied, each in his own manner, figures, gestures, drapery, foreshortening and groups. They looked, copied and understood.

In the hours left free from work and studies they fixed the day and the time for each new appointment, returning to the same subject until all of the pictorial experience of the Maestro had been transferred to the notes and drawings of his eager pupils.

«Tomorrow it's Masaccio, at the Carmine!».

After six months of diligently studying Giotto in Santa Croce, here they were packed together in the narrow Brancacci Chapel, gazing at one of the most striking frescos in the world. They studied shading, volumes, gestures, copying them bit by bit, questioning, analyzing, exchanging impressions, opinions and verdicts.

The young Buonarroti was not generous. He was the best, and he knew it. He felt no indulgence for the others, even the older ones. Barely glancing at their drawings he mocked them with the stinging Florentine sarcasm that cuts like a knife.

This went on until one morning Pietro Torrigiani, «envious of Michelangelo», says Vasari, «provoked by Buonarroti» according to others, went from words to action. Benevenuto Cellini described the incident as told him by Torrigiani himself:

«This Michelagnolo and I were going to learn as boys in the Church of the Carmine at the Chapel of Massaccio, and since Buonarroti used to mock everybody who was drawing, one day, when he was bothering me as well as the others, I was provoked more than usual and I grabbed his hand and gave him such a blow on the nose that I felt the bone crumble and the nose collapse under my fist like a doughnut; and he was marked for the rest of his life».

Michelangelo, states his biographer Condivi, «was carried home like a dead man», while all his friends begged «Torrigiano» to flee from the anger of Lorenzo.

The meeting

THE QUESTION SPRINGS TO MIND, what did Lorenzo de' Medici, the Magnificent Lorenzo, have to do with Michelangelo's nose?

Michelangelo, or more precisely Michelagnolo Buonarroti, was born in Caprese, a village in the valley of the Tiber, on March 6, 1475.

«I hereby record that today, on this 6th day of March 1474, a male child was born to me. I named him Michelagnolo, and he was born on Monday morning at about 4 or 5, and he was born when I was magistrate of Caprese...».

This record was left by Messer Lodovico di Leonardo Buonarroti Simoni, citizen of Florence, at the time magistrate of Chiusi and Caprese. The date of birth is wrong by one year since it was calculated according to the Florentine calendar. In Florence, in fact, the year began *ab incarnatione* (March 25), while according to the Roman calendar it was calculated *a nativitate* (December 25). For us then, definitively converted to the Roman calendar, Michelangelo was born in 1475.

Less than a month later Lodovico's term of office expired. In April he brought his family back to Florence and Michelangelo was put out to nurse with a woman who lived in Settignano, the daughter of one stonemason and the wife of another.

«Giorgio», Michelangelo, now an old man, was to say one day to Vasari, «if I have anything of genius, it came to me from being born in the keen sharp air of our town Arezzo; just as I drew in with my nurse's milk the chisels and the hammer that I use to make the figures».

Michelangelo's mother, Francesca di Ser Miniato del Sera, died young, probably when her second son was only about six years old. Lodovico married again, a woman called Lucrezia degli Ubaldini, to give his children a stepmother at least.

Michelangelo's first teacher was a certain Francesco da Urbino, a humanist who taught grammar in Florence, but the boy was an indifferent student. He learned to read and write, but certainly not the *donatello*, the first elements of Latin. «Heaven was calling me to draw and to work with painters», the artist was to confess later, «and could not be opposed».

Michelangelo's first friend was a painter, Francesco Granacci, a disciple of Domenico del Ghirlandaio. They must have met in 1486 or '87, when Michelangelo was about twelve years old and Granacci about eighteen.

«You want to paint, do you? I'll speak to your father and tell him to send you to Maestro Domenico's workshop. Here, take these drawings, you can have them. Copy them».

But for Lodovico Buonarroti art was disgraceful. He saw no difference between a painter and a whitewasher, between a stonemason and a sculptor.

«My father, and my father's brothers», the elderly Michelangelo was to recall sadly, «beat me hard and often, ashamed to think that art was entering the family». But nothing could make the boy turn back now. Encouraged by his friend Granacci, he rapidly went from drawing to painting and began to frequent Ghirlandaio's workshop.

«1488. On this first day of April I record how I Lodovico di Leonardo di Buonarota apprenticed Michelagnolo my son to Domenico and Davit di Tommaso di Currado for the next three years...».

It was done. His father, indignant but resigned, had given his consent. Now painting was no long forbidden fruit, but daily bread. In only a few months this boy of thirteen began to amaze his master. He drew with his own unique style, quite different from that of Ghirlandaio. Once he even corrected one of Maestro Domenico's drawings, outlining a woman's features with a heavier brushstroke that revealed the defects of the original. Then one day when everyone was busily at work on the scaffolding in the choir of Santa Maria Novella, he made an astoundingly realistic drawing of the scene: the scaffolding, the tools, the fresco, the painters and his young companions. Ghirlandaio, when he saw it, was forced to exclaim, «This one is really better than I am!».

One day Granacci showed Michelangelo a print by Martin Schongauer, a German forerunner of Dürer, depicting Saint Anthony raised aloft and tormented by nine devils in the form of monsters. The young Buonarroti was so struck by the drawing that he decided to copy it, painting it in colors. «And in portraying the demonic animals», relates Condivi, «he took such assiduous care that he colored nothing without first having taken note from nature. He went to a fish market, where he studied the shape and color of the fishes' fins, the color of their eyes and other parts, reproducing them in his painting; and so completing it as perfectly as he knew how, he won the admiration of everyone» and probably some envy as well, from Ghirlandaio.

«By Michelangelo? Of course, it's his too, but it does come from my workshop», repeated Maestro Domenico, attempting to take the credit for his disciple's talent.

Before a year was up Michelangelo had realized that he was not born to handle paintbrushes and colors. In Ghirlandaio's workshop he had found the chance to depict figures, but had also decided that his own means of expression, the one most suited to his temperament, was not painting but sculpture.

It may be that, like some remote memory of his childhood in Settignano, there arose in him the image of man and stone, the stonemason who imparts shape and light to the figure emerging from the rock; and judging fresco to be «not his art», he abruptly left Ghirlandaio's workshop to enter Bertoldo's sculpture garden.

Lorenzo de' Medici had collected a number of ancient works in the garden of San Marco, and had told Bertoldo to scout the workshops for young artists who wished to study sculpture. There were plenty of painters in Florence but now that Rossellino, Desiderio da Settignano, Donatello, Duccio, Mino da Fiesole, Luca della Robbia and Verrocchio were all dead, very few sculptors.

Michelangelo's meeting with Lorenzo was to be one of those mysterious appointments with fate that mark a turning point in the life of a man.

So laying aside his brushes, Michelangelo began to learn about marble and chisels.

As his first work he had decided to copy the time-worn head of a leering old faun. He succeeded so well that Maestro Bertoldo, unable to believe his eyes, had to show the sculpture to the Magnificent.

«Excellent», said Lorenzo, «truly excellent. But look, you've made an old faun and left all of his teeth in his mouth. Don't you know that old men are always missing a few?».

Upon his next visit to the garden Lorenzo the Magnificent saw the faun's head again. Now Michelangelo had not only removed an upper tooth from the mouth, but also bored the gums in strikingly realistic detail.

«Where is that boy?»

«He must be here somewhere, I saw him a few minutes ago», answered Bertoldo.

«Call him, have him come here».

When Michelangelo was before him, Lorenzo said:

«Tell your father that it would please me to speak to him tomorrow».

Lodovico was highly disturbed at this message. He didn't want to go. He couldn't stand the idea of having a son who was a stonemason. But Granacci soon convinced him by reminding him of who Lorenzo the Magnificent was and what it meant to contradict him.

The next day Messer Lodovico Buonarroti Simoni punctually appeared at the palace in Via Larga, and an agreement was reached.

Michelangelo was turned over to Lorenzo the Magnificent, who would keep him like a son. Lodovico was authorized to look around for some job he might like, and Lorenzo would help him to get it.

«Agreed, Lodovico?»

«Agreed? Not only Michelangelo but all the rest of us, with our life and our belongings, are at the disposal of Your Magnificence!».

In the home of the Magnificent

Lorenzo the Magnificent gave each of Bertoldo's pupils who worked in the sculpture garden of San Marco a salary adequate to his needs. Torrigiani, from a wealthy family, got enough to pay for his amusements and his vices; Giuliano Bugiardini, the son of poor people who lived far away beyond Porta a Faenza, received enough to give his family real help.

Michelangelo, who had now definitively moved from Via Bentaccordi to Via Larga, received five ducats a month. In addition, he had a bedroom as comfortable as could be desired in those days and a place at table, not as guest but as member of the household. Even more he was given a magnificent gift, a beautiful cloak of purple cloth.

This was Lorenzo, Michelangelo's new father; called «the Magnificent» because «Magnificent Messere» was the title conferred on the Gonfaloniers of the Republic, but remaining through the centuries «The Magnificent» because he alone, while still too young to be a gonfalonier, had had that attribute bestowed on him by the people and the government of Florence.

In a turbulent period of European politics, with the Pope, the King of France and the King of Spain jockeying for position, with the Italian Signorie seething in agitation and with Pisa bringing war up to the very gates of the city, Lorenzo had managed to make peace among all, compromising between their demands and claims so well that he was justly called «the needle in the scales of European balance». It was a balance not imposed, but skillfully sought and constructed, with that patience which often distinguishes great political action. At the risk of his life Lorenzo had gone to Naples, putting himself in the hands of his enemy, King Ferdinand of Aragon, the Pope's ally, to convince him through the force of logic and the clarity of good sense that a war would bring nothing but harm to both of them, inevitably provoking the interference of foreign powers. He had dared to challenge the rage and the excommunication of Sixtus IV. He had brought order back to Florence, giving his secret enemies a glimpse of the iron hand beneath the velvet glove. Like his grandfather Cosimo before him, he was loved and trusted by his people. He strolled through the streets without a bodyguard, pausing to chat with artisans, visiting the masters of art in their workshops or «on the bridges». They were all friends who knew they could count on him.

Lorenzo distributed no alms, but of the painters he ordered pictures and frescos, of the architects he demanded projects for palaces, fortresses and gardens, of the sculptors he asked statues for public squares and fountains for court-yards. To the scholars he proposed translations and comments on the classics, opening his precious library to them. In his home the most brilliant engineers of the time were welcomed like brothers. He respected his enemies, when they were honest like Savonarola. With poets he, himself a poet, spoke of poetry. With philosophers he, himself a philosopher, discoursed on man, God and the ultimate meaning of life. Lorenzo was truly the center and guiding spirit of that great movement known as «Florentine humanism» which was soon to blossom into the Italian Renaissance.

The first fruit Michelangelo's stay in the home of the Magnificent was a bas-relief, now known as *The Madonna of the Steps*, where the lesson learned from Donatello can still be seen. The Virgin is gentle and solemn, a woman without age and without time. The Child is like a little Hercules, turning toward his mother's breast in a twisting movement that emphasizes all of his muscles. More than a Madonna, the work seems to represent a Parca nursing an infant hero.

Although this bas-relief is small, slightly over a *braccio* in height, the proportions are gigantic. The artist's inclination for the grandiose and colossal was already emerging.

«Michelangelo, come to see me later; I'll translate for you the description of a battle that you will find interesting».

The humanist Agnolo Ambrogini, known as Poliziano, a poet who wrote in Greek and Latin as well as in Italian, felt real sympathy for that boy, always so quiet and attentive.

This was the origin, in a room of the palace in Via Larga, of Michelangelo's second bas-relief, which narrates in shapes and volumes the dramatic struggle of the centaurs for the beautiful Deianira. In this little masterpiece where figures mingle harmoniously in the tumult of battle, the fifteen-year-old Michelangelo already shows the unique imprint of his style.

The discussions of Pico della Mirandola, Marsilio Ficino, Poliziano, and Benevieni, animated and stimulated by the Magnificent, opened up to Michelangelo the doors of a marvelous unknown world, where man seeks and finds again a new and hitherto unsuspected dignity. Francesco da Urbino, his boyhood teacher, had not even tried to teach his pupil Latin and Greek; but now, in the palace on Via Larga, the humanists were speaking of the classic world as a reality which has its perfect match in real life. Ideas and concepts were discussed among them not in abstract terms but in words accessible to all. Michelangelo, listening, was unaware of nourishing himself with the highest thought of the neo-platonic school.

«Take that stone, for example. Do you see it? it's a piece of stone, unformed, representing nothing. And yet», explained the Canon Marsilio Ficino, «within it an idea is enclosed, a form is imprisoned. If a sculptor should remove little by little, with knowing skill, everything that is "too much", there would emerge from it, would be freed from it, a marvelous statue. It is not with the hands, my friends, that we paint or sculpt, but with the intellect!».

Michelangelo silently agreed with these remarks, meditated on them during the night and next morning, in the sculpture garden of San Marco, experimented with them in stone.

Even the finest artist has no concept
That the marble block itself does not contain
To release that form...

he was to write many years later, recalling the teachings of Marsilio, not knowing that this truth had been clearly enunciated twelve centuries before by Plotinus in the IV book of the *Enneads*.

That brotherhood of exceptional men was proposing for the first time, to future centuries, a humanity aware of its limitations but unwilling to bow its head before mystery. And apart from the venerable Marsilio Ficino they were all young men, not yet forty or, like Lorenzo, only a little older.

Their adversary was young too. He was a Dominican friar from Ferrara, newly come to Florence in the Monastery of San Marco.

He publicly commented the Old Testament, not treating it as an ancient text but reviving it, making it come alive in those who listened, as if it were the most modern of books. Sodom and Gomorra were not the destroyed cities of Babylon, but Rome and Florence, where those without scruples (the allusion to Lorenzo was obvious) were distracting men's souls with lust and sin, dragging them down to perdition.

The humanists, and even Lorenzo, went to San Marco or to the Duomo to hear the friar announcing in apocalyptic tones the punishment of God that was to fall on the city corrupted by art and new ideas.

The young Michelangelo heard those sermons that had the strange power of terrifying those who listened. In his heart he compared the scholarly discussions of his friends with the friar's crude preaching. As an artist he had no doubts. Art could only be nourished by intelligence and beauty, it could only unfold and flower around the Magnificent. But as a Christian, for whom life is only a moment of trial, he was forced to admit that Savonarola was right, that he was proclaiming again the vanity of all, the sinfulness of any idea or act which did not lead back to Christ.

Savonarola was the necessary antithesis of humanism. A conservative in the midst of innovators, he impersonated the desperate reaction of a now superseded world. His influence on his contemporaries was such that even a skeptical, erudite man like Pico della Mirandola felt obliged to hear him preach, and was deeply perturbed by what he heard.

Moreover, Savonarola was, in his Gothic, dogmatic absolutism, totally sincere. Lorenzo tried to threaten him, but in vain. He tried to corrupt him, but to no avail.

«Let him speak», concluded Lorenzo; «sooner or later he'll tire of it».

But the Prior of San Marco did not tire. And while Lorenzo opened the Carnival parades with their allegorical floats inspired by mythology and the populace rushed to the Cascine to celebrate the great feast with singing and libations, Savonarola in the Monastery of San Marco was already preparing the future processions of the faithful who, strewing ashes on their hair, were soon to challenge the carnival songs with penitential ones chanted to the same meter, exalting mortification and calling for repentance.

Michelangelo stayed three years in the palace on Via Larga. And if he made only two bas-reliefs in all that time, it is certain that he not only studied in Bertoldo's sculpture garden but also listened, read, questioned and nourished his soul at that font of knowledge that was to make of him the great conciliator between the classic and the modern world, between the pagan and the Christian message.

On April 8, 1492, Lorenzo de' Medici lay dying in his villa of Careggi. He had been sick for months and everyone in the palace on Via Larga was anxiously observing the course of the illness. Lorenzo's father had died at the age of forty-eight of the same disease, gout, that was to kill his son at forty-three.

It was a stormy Spring. On the night between April 5th and 6th during a furious thunderstorm six bolts of lightning had struck the lantern on the top of the Duomo, breaking several columns.

Lorenzo, already far gone, asked on which side the columns had fallen. They told him, and he murmured:

«Alas, they fell toward my house. This time it's really the end».

Pico della Mirandola and Poliziano took turns watching over him. But his death was then and still remains today obscure. According to Poliziano, on the night of the 7th Father Guido dei Camaldolesi, Lorenzo's confessor, arrived, gave him absolution and administered to him the sacraments. According to the Dominicans instead, as reported by Fra' Silvestro Maruffi, later burned at the stake with Savonarola, what happened was very different, more dramatic and also more in keeping with the personalities of the Magnificent and of his antagonist.

On the morning of April 8th, having lost all hope of recovery, Lorenzo said:

«Bring me Father Girolamo, because I have never found a real friar but him».

The Prior of San Marco went immediately to Careggi, where Lorenzo told him he wanted to confess.

«Before I hear your confession», said Savonarola, «you must promise three things, being certain of salvation if you fulfill them. In the first place, Lorenzo», continued the Dominican, «you must have great faith».

«That I have immensely», answered the dying man.

«In the second place you must give back all of your illegitimately acquired property».

Lorenzo, after reflecting a moment, replied, «Father, I wish to do so at any cost and to oblige my heirs to do so».

«Third», continued Savonarola, always more demanding, «you must restore liberty to the republic and reinstate its old constitution».

In a single instant, as in an immense present, Lorenzo saw his whole existence spent for the greatness of Florence, from the death of his father to that of his brother; saw the city as it was when he had received it and as it was now: industrious, wealthy, civilized, in the vanguard, the leader in a general re-awakening that had attracted the attention and respect of the known world; cultured and refined for the geniuses who animated it and the artists who showed their love of it in enduring masterpieces. He saw the disastrous consequences of the return of the factions, the explosion of hate and revenge. And without deigning to reply to the last demand of this friar from another land, he turned his head away and died.

Outside the storm raged. A hurricane of wind and water tore through the woods around Careggi. By torch light the family secretly brought Lorenzo's body to the city to place it in the Monastery of San Marco. That same night Lorenzo's doctor threw himself, or was thrown, into a well.

From Careggi, news of the death quickly reached Via Larga, echoed through the city, and spread throughout the world.

«*Ecce gladius Domini super terram, cito et velociter*», had cried the Dominican friar from the pulpit.

«Now the peace of Italy is broken», declared, with painful certainty, Pope Innocent VIII.

«This man was, in the opinion of the world, the most glorious man alive» wrote in his diary the humble tradesman Luca Landucci.

In the hearts of many, and in that of Michelangelo in particular, time and life had abruptly come to a halt, as if petrified.

The statue made of snow

ON JANUARY 20, 1494 (1493 by the Florentine calendar)
«it snowed in Florence the greatest snow that can ever
be remembered». The snowstorm went on for twenty-four
hours without a break, and the city was paralyzed.

In the Medici palace the young Piero, confirmed by the
Signoria as Lorenzo's successor, viewing that extraordinary
sight, sent for Michelangelo to have him make a beautiful
statue of snow down in the courtyard.

Michelangelo no longer lived in the palace in Via Larga.
After the death of the Magnificent he had gone back to his
father's house in Via Bentaccordi, grieving so deeply that he
had been unable to work for weeks. He lived in a daze, speaking with no one. Lorenzo de' Medici had been his real father,
his guardian angel. Now he felt a wound in his soul. But he
was seventeen years old, and at that age healing is necessary
and natural. Conquering his grief he had bought a great block
of marble which had been exposed for years to the weather,
and begun to sculpt in it a *Hercules* four *braccia* tall.

The snowfall of January 20th took him by surprise as he
was intent on finishing his statue.

«Michelangelo, come to the palace at once, Piero is calling for you!».

Michelangelo went upstairs to change. His stingy old father
Lodovico, seeing him by now «almost always in the company
of grown men», had «dressed him with more decent clothes».
Throwing over his shoulders the purple cloak given him by
Lorenzo he made his way through the snow to Via Larga.

«Come, Michelangelo, you must make me a beautiful
statue of snow!».

Should this be considered once again an insult to genius?
Rivers of ink have flowed over this statue, but it must be

viewed within the context of the times. Piero was twenty, Michelangelo seventeen; two boys who had lived together as brothers. So nothing could be more natural than that request. Michelangelo was a sculptor, and even more, he was the family sculptor.

Michelangelo willingly accepted the job. It was customary in Florence, on those rare occasions when it snowed, to have sculptors make statues in the snow, the Marzocco being a favorite subject, just as painters made banners for processions and tournaments.

Michelangelo made a statue so big and beautiful that Piero was delighted. In a sudden burst of sympathy, or perhaps remorse, he told his friend to come back and live in the palace again, with the same room and the same place at table.

So Michelangelo went back to Via Larga. He finished the statue of *Hercules* and sold it to Alfonso Strozzi. It ended up in the hands of the French king Francis I. Today the fate of the *Hercules* is unknown. No one has seen it, no one knows anything about it. It remained in the gardens of Fontainebleau up to the early 18th century. Then it disappeared.

From the Medici palace Michelangelo began to frequent the Augustinian monastery of Santo Spirito, whose prior had given him «the convenience of a room» in which «to skin corpses» in order to study their anatomy and perfect himself still further in drawing.

This was of course not only prohibited, but considered sacrilege. The Monastery of Santo Spirito supported a small hospice for the poor and sick of the Oltrarno quarter. Before being buried, the dead were studied by the young sculptor, who went to the monastery by night, unknown to all except the prior, his friend and accomplice.

The wooden crucifix still hanging in the Sacristy of Santo Spirito is a copy of the lost original, an indirect expression of the sculptor's gratitude.

This was the first as well as the last time that Michelangelo worked in a material that was not made for him.

Life in the Medici Palace might have seemed the same as in the time of Lorenzo had Piero not been so superficial. Inconstant and easily swayed, he was known as «Piero the Fatuous». Today young men like this, likable but frivolous, can be found everywhere. They are the gilded youth who have the misfortune of knowing they can have whatever they want, and are sure they can buy anything, even friendship.

Michelangelo was considered the family genius. Piero spoke highly of him, but in the same words he used in boasting of an extraordinary Spanish groom. He put them on the same level, describing them as two «phenomena». The groom, in addition to being as beautiful as a classical statue, could run so fast that Piero, galloping on his horse, could not outdistance him by a yard.

At table there was, in addition to Piero, his brother Giovanni, the same age as Michelangelo, secretly appointed cardinal when he was fourteen years old and officially proclaimed the year before. Then there was Giuliano, the youngest of Lorenzo's sons, and Contessina, the only daughter not yet married, three years younger than Michelangelo. Contessina was a radiant, ethereal figure, a thin pale girl who seemed all eyes and ardent emotion. Michelangelo's silent affection for her can easily be imagined. There was still Poliziano, continuing to open up to him the classical world, reading to him the Greek poets and Plato; and the Count of Mirandola, and the erudite Benivieni. And there was Cardiere, the lute-player who used to entertain Lorenzo the Magnificent in the evenings, improvising songs to the music of his lyre.

«Michelangelo, I had a terrible dream last night! Lorenzo appeared before me. He was dressed in black, with a torn jacket over his bare breast. And he told me: "Cardiere, go to my son Piero and tell him that he will soon be driven out of Florence, never to return!". What must I do?»

«Go to Piero, just as Lorenzo ordered you to».

But Cardiere was afraid. He had confided only in Michelangelo, since he had to tell somebody, but he feared to face Piero's arrogance.

A few days later, while Michelangelo was in the courtyard, Cardiere appeared again, his face grey with fear. Calling Michelangelo to one side, he trembled as he told him:

«Again last night! I saw him again last night. He was dressed in black, his clothes all torn as before. And I felt I was not asleep, I was awake, I saw him. Lorenzo came up to me, and glowering at me he slapped me hard because I hadn't given Piero his message!».

Michelangelo grabbed Cardiere by the shirt front. Shaking him hard, he exhorted him to remember that the voice of a dead soul was God's command. At last he persuaded Cardiere to take the road for Careggi, where Piero was staying with his friends.

Half-way there Cardiere met the company on its way back to the city. Approaching Piero he told him he had a secret message for him, then whispered into his ear what he had seen and heard.

Piero broke out in a hearty laugh. He called his friends around him and told them the sinister prediction. Then lifting his foot from the stirrup and placing it on the messenger's neck he gave a shove, ordering his footmen to take a few good kicks at that bird of ill omen.

When Michelangelo heard of the welcome given his friend he had no more doubts. He went to Alfonso Strozzi, who had offered to buy the marble *Hercules*, and concluded the affair. Then, having secretly informed his father Lodovico, he left the Medici Palace by night with two companions (one of them was perhaps Granacci, the other Cardiere himself) and left for Venice. It was early October of 1494. The young Contessina had married Piero Ridolfi four months ago and gone to live in Rome. Poliziano, the only friend Michelangelo had left, had died a few days earlier, between the 28th and 29th of September; died of unrequited love.

Less than a month later, on November 9th, 1494, a Sunday, Piero di Lorenzo de' Medici was driven out of Florence at the cry of «The People and Liberty», and a price of two thousand ducats was placed on his head.

The wax seal

T HE THREE YOUNG men arrived at the gates of Bologna in the afternoon. There was a long line of people waiting at the customs office. Instead of stopping like everybody else they went right on and entered the city, looking for an inn. In a narrow alley at the heart of the city they saw a sign to their liking, tied their horses to the rings fixed in the wall and entered.

«We are foreigners, we come from Venice. Have you got a room with three beds?»

«Certainly, messere. Have you got a visa?».

Two men in uniform who were sitting near the doorway got up and approached Michelangelo.

«Please show me your hands», said the one who seemed to be in charge. Michelangelo and his friends held out their hands.

«You have no seal», said the gendarme.

«What seal?»

«All those who enter the city, except citizens of Bologna, are required to have a seal of red wax applied to the right thumbnail. You haven't obeyed this order so I must ask you to follow me to the license office».

Michelangelo and his two friends were taken to the law court and sentenced to pay fifty Bolognese coins each for not having respected the orders of Giovanni Bentivoglio, the suspicious lord of Bologna.

«But we are artists, we don't have that much money», said Michelangelo.

«Then you can sleep in prison».

Standing nearby was a gentleman of Bologna, a member of the Council of Sixteen, the governing body of the city.

«Just a moment», he said. «You say you are artists. Can you tell me something more?».

Michelangelo spoke for himself, told him who he was and what he had done; explained that he had left Florence before Piero had been driven out, that he had gone to Venice and been forced to come back because life in that city was too expensive, and that he had entered Bologna without anyone telling him he had to have his fingernail stamped.

The gentleman, who was called Gianfrancesco Aldovrandi, saw that he was speaking to an honest, truthful person. Moreover, he vaguely recalled having heard speak of the young Buonarroti by his Florentine humanist friends. He offered to help with the license office and invited Michelangelo to his home.

The sculptor did not want to leave his two friends.

«They live on my money», he said.« How can I abandon them?».

Aldovrandi, smiling, asked him:

«Michelangelo, can I join your company too? If you want to take people wandering around the world and pay all their expenses, why should I stay here in Bologna? I'm coming with you».

Michelangelo apologized to his two friends who had overheard this conversation. Emptying his pockets, he gave them everything he had left, and followed Aldovrandi.

Having just come from Venice, Michelangelo did not know that Piero de' Medici with all his followers had taken refuge precisely in Bologna; but his host and protector knew it, and for this reason trusted the young fugitive immediately.

Michelangelo stayed with Aldovrandi for over a year. The gentleman of Bologna liked him at once, recognized his great talent, and wanted his city to benefit by it.

He showed Michelangelo the tomb of San Domenico, in the church dedicated to that saint, left unfinished by Niccolò Pisano. There was an angel missing, and a Saint Proculus and a Saint Petronius by Niccolò da Bari to be finished. Did Michelangelo dare try to make them? He replied that he did, and Aldovrandi used his authority to have the unknown Florentine sculptor assigned the task of completing those statues, for a recompense of thirty ducats.

Michelangelo, supplied with marble and tools, began to work on the angels and saints on the tomb. In the evenings, his day's work completed, he read to the gentlemen from Bologna Dante's *Divine Comedy* and Boccaccio's *Decameron*, since Aldovrandi, himself a poet and humanist, liked to hear poetry read by a Tuscan.

When the statues were finished and put in their proper places, Michelangelo felt the hate of a Bolognese sculptor who had wanted to sculpt them himself. Michelangelo's work was of such high quality that the clients felt no regret for what the Bolognese sculptor might have been able to accomplish. Talk of revenge was soon followed by threats of death.

Michelangelo was not one to pick a fight. On the contrary, he was fearful by nature, and decided once again to flee, to return to Florence where he would feel secure.

Aldovrandi understood the feelings of his young friend and let him go. It was Autumn of 1495. In Florence, after Piero de' Medici had been driven out, an invisible king governed. He had been proclaimed and crowned by Savonarola: his name was Jesus Christ.

The cry of a capon among a hundred cocks

A NYONE WHO RETURNS home after a year away, without having been able to send news or receive it, apart from the minimum indispensable to say that he is alive and in good health, will want to question friends and family members, to get an idea of the past and present reality, putting it together piece by piece like a mosaic.

And much had happened in Florence in the last year.

Michelangelo pieced together the events of those days, gathering news from all around him, since everyone was talking about these still fresh happenings.

«You see, Michelangelo», stated the prudent Lodovico,«this is what the masses are like. Today they light torches in your honor, like that evening of Piero de' Medici's return from Pisa, and the next day they are looting your palace».

In spite of his arrogance Piero had, in fact, understood better than the Signoria that the King of France must be kept a friend. When on October 4th the ambassadors of Charles VIII urgently demanded permission to pass through Florentine territory, the Signoria had answered in its usual way, hedging and hesitating.

«We're not saying no», they answered.

«But not yes either!», replied the others; and indignantly returned to the king, who swore he would abandon Florence to be plundered by his soldiers.

«And who went to make peace with Charles VIII?», commented Giuliano Bugiardini. «It was Piero de' Medici and Lorenzo Tornabuoni. Piero offered the King of France, who had already occupied Sarzana, the castles of Sarzanello and Pietrasanta. The French king wanted confirmation by the Signoria, and Lorenzo Tornabuoni was sent to get it from them in writing».

But the Signoria, incited by Piero's cousins, who had just been exiled to a place a mile outside of the city walls for conspiracy, refused to confirm anything. Lorenzo Tornabuoni, disheartened, could not find the courage to go before the king again, and Piero de' Medici took the blame.

On the 4th of November a decree issued by the Signoria obliged all Florentines to open their homes to the royal quartermasters to provide lodgings for the French. The quartermasters entered the city, inspected all of the houses one by one, counting the beds and marking signs in chalk on the walls and doors of each dwelling to indicate the name and rank of those who would lodge there.

«This one is for the captain, that one for the baron. Not hundreds, but thousands of houses were requisitioned».

A few days late Florence was overflowing with French officers.

«Open up here, open up there. They entered as patrons, saying they would pay, but there were few who put their hand to their purse. And those who paid something, paid for the horns and ate the ox».

With women instead they were courteous and well-mannered, as befitted the gallant knights of France.

«But», added Bugiardini,«in these days, as you know, a new evil is spreading far and wide, bringing swellings as in the plague, and they say it comes from them and they call it "the French evil"».

The advance troops of Charles VIII had entered Florence with plunder in their hearts. At the last moment instead, most of the army had remained with the king's retinue, and those who were lodged in the city felt besieged, in the midst of one hundred thousand Florentines ready to gather at the clanging of a bell. On the evening of November 8th Piero returned from Pisa. To celebrate his coming they lighted torches from the San Frediano Gate to the heart of the city. Arriving home, Piero had wine and cakes distributed to the people who thronged his courtyard to shout their welcome.

On the next day, which was a Sunday, Piero wanted to go to the Signoria, or was perhaps summoned by them, it is now unclear. It is certain however that the Signoria wanted him alone and unarmed; and that he came home again. But in the meanwhile, as if at a secret order, people suddenly began to stream from every street toward the square, to the cry of «The People and Liberty». The bells pealed to summon them. The Gonfalone was brought out, and behind it was Francesco Valori on horseback, accompanied by many armed men, all crying «The People and Liberty!».

Piero had taken refuge in his palace. With him was the Tornabuoni family and many other citizens faithful to the Medici. They quickly armed and rushed into the street crying «Balls! Balls!». Piero gave the signal and was leading them toward Piazza della Signoria when he suddenly realized that most of his followers had abandoned him and gone over to the other side, joining in the cry «The People and Liberty!».

Piero, followed by a few friends, swung his horse about and galloped toward the San Gallo gate, where his brother Giuliano awaited him with a group of armed men. Together they left the city, galloping in the direction of Bologna.

The young *cardinalino* Giovanni de' Medici, left alone in the palace on Via Larga, was seen from nearby windows kneeling on the floor, his hands joined in prayer, fervently entreating God. He was also seen, disguised as a monk, making his way between the palace and the monastery of San Marco to put the precious manuscripts from the library of the Magnificent in a safe place. Then, still disguised, he too escaped from Florence.

The palace on Via Larga was devastated by the people. Works of art, furniture, decorations, tapestries, silverware, porcelain, brocades, manuscripts, arms and trappings were snatched away with the fury of vandals.

«Under penalty of the gallows» the Signoria issued a band ordering the citizens to denounce «whoever had, or whoever knew that others had, objects and property stolen from the home of the Medici». But by now it was too late, the evil was done.

It took years of patient searching to find, scattered all over the world, the objects not destroyed at the time, which are today conserved in the museums of Florence.

In the meantime Charles VIII was approaching Florence, escorted by a guard of 200 horsemen, followed by 10,000 lancers, 8,000 harquebusiers, 12,000 crossbowmen, 8,000 Swiss infantrymen and the entire artillery.

On November 16th great preparations were being made for the arrival of the king, especially in the home of Piero de' Medici where he was to be lodged. As the palace built by Michelozzo seemed too severe and unadorned, two great columns were erected before the entrance, decorated with the lilies of France, surrounded by statues of cupids and giants, allegories of victory and honors.

The people of Florence were capable of this too. Only a week before, in an excess of rebellious fury, they had avenged their disappointment with the Medici family in destruction. Now, called upon to display their best for the arrival of an illustrious guest, they had transformed the city in a single night, veiling its wounds, arraying it in the guise of fantasy.

«Long live France!», cried the people, while the barons on horseback paraded by, solemn in their richly embroidered garments, with their priceless saddles and finely chiseled arms. It took more than two hours for them to reach the cathedral from the San Frediano Gate.

The young king of France proved a disappointment to the Florentines, who were expecting something better. Charles VIII was small but not handsome, courteous but not cordial.

He took possession of the Medici palace and on the next day opened negotiations with the Signoria. It was a give and take lasting many days. Every so often, at the cry of «Lock up! Lock up!», the people barricaded themselves in their houses ready for defense. Then the news turned out to be a false alarm, and doorways and shops opened up again. But every night left its toll of dead men lying in the dark alleyways, now from one side, now from the other.

The turning point came when the king, exhorted by Savonarola to leave, set conditions judged unacceptable by the Signoria.

Pier Capponi, who was ambassador for the Florentines, risked his life, tearing the paper on which those hard conditions were written into pieces in the presence of the king. Outraged at this, the king shouted his famous words:«*We will sound our trumpets!*» and Capponi replied with the even more famous ones: «*And we our bells!*».

But that was exactly what neither of the two adversaries really wanted.

On November 26th, after long, hard negotiations, the king and the whole Signoria heard mass together in Santa Maria del Fiore, and Charles VIII swore to respect the agreements reached, namely:

«Florence would lend him, or better give him, since repayment was not contemplated, 120,000 golden florins;

«Charles VIII, upon his return to France, would give back to the Florentines Pisa and all the castles;

«Piero de' Medici remained banned from the city, forbidden to come within 100 miles of Florence;

«The price placed on his head and on that of his brothers was annulled».

Two days later the bells did sound, but in festive celebration. The joyful peals accompanied the King of France, echoing from one bell-tower to the next as far as the Certosa. The French army was leaving the city of the flower and the houses marked with chalk «as if they had just been passing through».

In his modest home Machiavelli noted:

The clamor of arms and of horses
Could not drown out
The cry of a capon among a hundred cocks.

The Weepers and the Angry Ones

«MICHELANGELO, I WANT you to work for me too», said Lorenzo de' Medici. «I saw your *Hercules* in the Strozzi palace and I must have something of yours. What about a young Saint John?».

Lorenzo di Pierfrancesco de' Medici, a cousin of the Magnificent, proclaimed himself the friend of the people. Exiled by Lorenzo, he had returned at his death, rivaling Piero in adventures of the heart and plotting against him in political ones. Restricted to his splendid villa of Castello, at the gates of Florence, he had returned after the expulsion of Piero and had been appointed one of the twenty reformers in the San Giovanni quarter of the city.

Like the Magnificent, he was the friend of humanists and artists. Although he had repudiated the name of «Medici» to assume that of «Popolani», he remained a highly refined collector of works of art, detesting vulgarity of any kind.

Michelangelo was glad to accept this commission. Although the *young Saint John* greatly pleased his client the statue was soon to disappear, how or where no one knows, and is lost to this day.

Lorenzo ordered another work from Michelangelo, a God of Love lying down to sleep, the size of a six-year-old child. The finished statue was so perfect that Lorenzo constantly compared it to the masterpieces of classical art.

«If the marble were old, and not so white, it would deceive anyone. Michelangelo, why don't you try burying it in the ground to age it, so we could pass it off as an antique?».

Michelangelo was not a counterfeiter, but he liked the idea of hoodwinking the so-called experts. He gave the statue a special treatment, so skillfully applied that it seemed at least twenty centuries old, though well preserved.

Then at the suggestion of Lorenzo he sent it to Rome, to a certain Baldassarre del Milanese who acted as go-between in the sale of objects from excavations or, as we would say today, as art merchant.

Upon receiving the *Cupid* Baldassare showed it at once to the Cardinal of San Giorgio, Raffaele Riario, declaring that this jewel of classical art had been recently dug up in a vineyard.

The cardinal, having examined the statue, decided to buy it for two hundred ducats. The merchant sent Michelangelo thirty ducats, writing that he had been unable to get more for it.

In the meantime, from the pulpits of Santa Maria del Fiore and San Marco, Savonarola was the de facto ruler of the city. A year before, in the critical hour of Piero's flight and the return of the exiles, he had preached against revenge, calling for peace and forgiveness.

«Peace, I say, peace, Florence!», he cried, his voice broken with emotion. «Hear, Florence, what I say to you this morning. From you will come forth the reformation of all Italy!».

He examined the text of the new constitution, suggesting supplements and amendments but urging the city to conclude it and make it executive now, leaving the finishing touches to be added by experience.

«I have told you before, Florence, that it is better to have only one head who governs. Hearken, O Florence, God wants to content you and give you one head and one king. And this is Christ!».

«This evil friar will bring us trouble», the citizens began to murmur. «He meddles too much in politics, is too sure of being inspired by God».

«Lionardo», said Michelangelo one day to this brother, who had become a Dominican friar and had returned to San Marco from the monastery at Pisa, «be careful. I heard just this morning that the Pope has ordered Friar Girolamo to stop preaching».

But the Dominican friar, after some days of silence, began again more vehemently that ever. At Carnival time in 1496 he launched his great offensive of the *fanciugli*, interminable processions bearing banners, trumpets, fifes and maces, in which only males could participate. Women, of any age and condition, had to stay at home. They were even forbidden to show themselves at window or door. The marchers in the procession carried olive branches in their hands and sang loud hymns of praise to the Virgin and to Christ.

Frequently, however, fanatic devotion transformed those heavenly boys into raging demons. Spurred on by the friar, they felt themselves the guardians of public morality, entering hostels to overturn gamblers' tables, assaulting and beating women who, in their opinion, were not dressed modestly enough. On one occasion a girl who was walking home accompanied by her parents had her veil torn off and was roughly pushed about, guilty in their eyes of being too elegant. They even searched houses. Entering in gangs, bullying their way, they confiscated everything deemed insufficiently sober, a lovely dress, a picture inspired by mythology, a frivolous book, a mirror, feminine ornaments like bracelets and necklaces, scarves and veils. All these things were piled up in Piazza della Signoria, to be burnt in those fires that the friar called «bonfires of vanity».

«It can't last», murmured the people, more and more of them, louder and louder.

«It's not quiet enough to work», thought Michelangelo, watching his brother Lionardo hurrying back and forth between home and San Marco, now having risen almost to the rank of deputy to Savonarola.

«The Weepers» was the name given the friar's followers.

«The Angry Ones» were the others, those who hated the preaching rallies, faithfully attended by the ferocious boys who sat together in special stands.

«And on the 15th day of August, preached Friar Girolamo in Santa Maria del Fiore and, due to the crowd of people, one of those boys' stands collapsed, toward the gate of San Giovanni, and no one was hurt. This was held to be a miracle».

«And at this time Florence and the countryside around it were already full of the French boils, and they were in every city all over Italy and lasted a great time. Some medicated them and they shrank, gave great pains in all the joints, and finally went away. And no cure was to be found. Not many perished, but they dragged themselves about with great pains and foulness».

«And others there were, like a poor peasant who came to Florence to beg for bread, and left at home three children with no bread, and returning home found these children dying, and as he could not be comforted, he took a trestle and hung himself».

The Signoria, fearing epidemic, famine and rioting, decreed that no order of friars could preach without having obtained a regular permit. To this Savonarola replied by preaching in San Marco and exhorting his followers to «write for all and among the infidels, that there was in Florence a friar who was speaking the reform of the Church», and added: «Write this too; that it is God who says so!»

«Michelangelo, someone is looking for you», said Lodovico to his son one day, «it seems they have searched everywhere before finding our door».

A stranger entered the house of the young Michelangelo.

«I don't know your name», he said, but I know you are a sculptor».

Michelangelo expected his visitor to offer him work, since he added:

«I'd like to see something you have done to be sure».

Michelangelo had nothing. He rose in silence, took an ink-well, a pen, a sheet of paper, sat down next to the stranger and drew, with a few swift strokes, a perfect hand.

The gentlemen, amazed and satisfied, told him that he had been sent to Florence by the Cardinal of San Giorgio, in search of a Florentine sculptor who had carved a sleeping Cupid.

«Then I'm the one you're looking for», answered Michelangelo. «That figure is mine. I was commissioned to do it by Messer Lorenzo de' Medici and then I sent it to Rome to a certain Baldassarre del Milanese».

«Then you know», added the gentlemen, «that this Baldassarre has sold your statue to the Cardinal of San Giorgio, passing it off as antique and making him pay two hundred ducats».

«Two hundred ducats?», exclaimed Michelangelo. «I have a letter in which Baldassare had me paid thirty ducats here in Florence, saying he been unable to get more and not telling me who bought it».

Michelangelo now realized that he had been tricked by the go-between, but not he alone. He was in good company, that of Cardinal Riario and Lorenzo de' Medici.

«Why don't you come to Rome with me?», said the stranger, adding that he would be glad to offer Michelangelo the hospitality of his home. He described the advantages of that great city where each individual could show what he was worth, certain that he would be judged on merit alone. Lastly, he assured Michelangelo of the benevolence of the Cardinal of San Giorgio, who would make that swindler Baldassarre pay him the difference of a hundred and seventy ducats, and even more important, would commission some great work from him. The messenger was so persuasive that Michelangelo asked only a few days to decide; but in his heart the decision was already made.

A signature by night

CARDINAL RAFFAELE RIARIO, nephew of the late Sixtus IV and protégé of Alexander VI, was young, extremely wealthy and smugly self-satisfied. When Michelangelo met him he was thirty-five years old, and the architects were just finishing his sumptuous palace known today as the Cancelleria. He was the friend and protector of humanists and a passionate art collector, though by no means an expert. As long as Michelangelo's *Cupid* had been a piece of classical sculpture it was a masterpiece. When the name of its real sculptor was known, it became worthless in his eyes. The Cardinal had become furious when he discovered the trick played on him. He had had Baldassare apprehended and demanded that he return the two hundred ducats, after which he gave him back the statue.

Michelangelo in turn, having found the merchant, demanded that he pay the difference. But Baldassare, who had reluctantly had to return the whole amount to the Cardinal of San Giorgio, exploded in anger, refusing not only to spend any more money, but also to give back the marble statue.

«Magnificent Lorenzo», wrote Michelangelo from Rome, «just to let you know that last Saturday we arrived at salvation».

What a trip from Florence to Rome meant in those days is hard to imagine now. Traveling by post, with carts that changed horses every eight hours, the trip took six or seven days. The roads were treacherous; armies, advancing or retreating, invaded them blocking all traffic; bands of armed cutthroats assaulted villages and inns, robbing the unlucky travelers of everything they had. No one brought money on his person, depositing it at a *banco* in the city he departed from and withdrawing it at an associated bank upon his arrival. The end of the trip meant the end of serious danger. Only when he had finally arrived did the traveler feel he had reached «salvation».

«We went at once to visit Cardinal San Giorgio», continued Michelangelo, «and gave him your letter. He seemed glad to see me, and wanted me to go immediately to see some statues. Then the Cardinal demanded whether I had it in me to make some beautiful work myself. I answered that I might not make such great works as he possessed, but he would see what I could do. We bought a piece of marble and on Monday I began work».

Humility and greatness do not resemble, but are at times the contrary, of modesty and conceit. Michelangelo was often humble, never modest; always aware of his own greatness, and never conceited.

From the letter to Lorenzo it can be guessed how that conversation with Cardinal Riario took place. The high prelate showed the sculptor the statues in his collection, also as an indication of what he wanted. Then he asked the sculptor if he «felt it in him» to create a statue worthy of that collection. Michelangelo answered that he did. He was ready to measure himself against those ancient masters. The results would be seen and judged later.

In the same letter Michelangelo describes the stormy meeting with Baldassarre: «... and I asked him for the little boy, and said I would give him back his money. He answered me very sharply, saying he would sooner smash it into a hundred piece, and that he had bought the boy and it was his ...».

That *Cupid* ended up in the hands of Duke Valentino, who gave it to the Marchioness of Mantua; and at Mantua it remained until all trace of it was lost.

Cardinal San Giorgio was a shining example of the fact that being rich and collecting masterpieces is not the same as loving and understanding art. He had been tricked by the merchant, and had to punish him. But he did not have to punish Michelangelo by refusing a work that even then was worth not two hundred, but two thousand ducats. And the sculptor suffered at this. Offended by the stinginess that humiliated him as artist, he expected very little from the Cardinal, and in fact got very little or nothing. The marble mentioned in the letter was bought, but the statue was never begun. Perhaps Riario had him sculpt a frieze for his palace, perhaps not even this. He looked on Michelangelo as his «art expert», the advisor to a Croesus arrayed as prince of the Church.

To add to Michelangelo's bitterness during that period of forced idleness was his meeting with the exiled Piero de' Medici. The son of the Magnificent, his heart filled with rage, his soul consecrated to a single end, that of returning to Florence and revenging himself on his enemies, revealed an inexplicable desire to have Michelangelo make him a statue. Where would he put it? Probably he intended to give it to some potential ally. It is known that Michelangelo took this offer seriously, although the statue was never made.

«I accepted», he wrote embittered to his father Lodovico, «to make a figure for Piero de' Medici and I bought the marble; but I have not started it since he has not given me what he promised; and for this reason I keep to myself ...».

Not just a way of behaving, but a rule of life is already clearly stated in this youthful phrase. From then on, up to the end of his long existence, the solitary Michelangelo was to have only his own company, to keep to himself.

But in Rome there were others besides Cardinal San Giorgio and Piero de' Medici. Others, with no less authority but much greater competence, were lovers of art and sought the friendship of artists. Jacopo Galli, a Roman gentleman and banker by profession, who lived near Palazzo Riario, was one of these. He soon made the acquaintance of Michelangelo, becoming a sincere admirer and inviting the artist to live in his home, with a room of his own and a study to work in. The first result of this fortunate encounter was the statue of *Bacchus*, now in the Bargello Museum at Florence.

The manner of treating the marble was probably the same as that of the lost *Cupid*: skillful smoothing, the refinement of every anatomical detail to transform stone into flesh and to give the statue the dreamy, stupefied attitude of a young man drunk on wine. It is a figure ten palms high, slightly over life size, representing a youth, classically perfect, «corresponding in every detail to the meaning intended by the ancient writers, with joyous face and sidelong, lascivious eyes. In his right hand he holds a cup, like one about to drink, gazing at it intently, like one who takes pleasure in that liquor, which he was the first to discover; in recognition of which his head is adorned with a garland of grapevines. In his left hand he holds the skin of a tiger, an animal dedicated to him, as it so greatly delights in the grape; and he showed the skin rather than the animal, intending to signify that he who loses himself in sensuality and the appetite for that fruit and the liquor made from it, will in the end lose his life. In the hand of this arm Bacchus holds a bunch of grapes, which a lithe and merry little satyr, placed at his feet, is furtively eating...».

This description, with the allegorical meanings, must have come from the mouth of the sculptor himself, so faithfully does the pupil Condivi repeat the words of his master.

Then, again for his bountiful host, Michelangelo made

another *Cupid*, which is now lost; but the friendship between Michelangelo and Jacopo Galli was not to be lost.

«And I Jacobo Galli promise to the most reverend Monsignor that the aforesaid Michelangelo will make the aforesaid work within one year and it will be the most beautiful work in marble to be found in Rome and no master will make a better one».

Much more than a promissory note, this is a blind commitment. Such a guarantee could never be signed through friendship alone, but only in the total conviction that the man in question is a genius, unrivaled among his contemporaries.

Jacopo Galli had heard that the Cardinal of Saint Denis, a French Benedictine named Jean Bilhères de Lagraulas, wanted to adorn the chapel of the King of France in Saint Peter's with a statue, perhaps in memory of his friend Charles VIII who had recently died at an early age. Galli offered to put at his disposal the only sculptor capable of creating a work deserving of such munificence.

Michelangelo was presented to the Cardinal, a recompense was agreed upon, four hundred and fifty gold ducats, and a contract was stipulated in which Jacopo Galli participated as witness and guarantee for the Cardinal and for Michelangelo.

This was the origin of the *Pietà*, the one now in Saint Peter's. Words cannot describe it. It can and must be seen.

The *Madonna of the Steps* is distinguished by a certain solemn, grave stillness, and in the other early works, including *Bacchus*, the classical lesson is clearly apparent. But in this marble group, the *Pietà*, there is only the imprint of genius, like the wellspring of a new expressive language, with the certain promise of the great works to come in the artist's maturity.

He had skinned the dead in Santo Spirito and studiously observed the corpses. Now the body of Christ, lying abandoned across the Virgin's knees, is really a dead body, with slackened nerves and muscles. It is inanimate flesh in the lap of a mother who is alive, but dead within. Maria's grief has no tears, her face is not torn by desperation, yet tragedy is in the gesture of her hands, in her lowered head, in her lap opening out in ample drapery to receive and shelter the body of her son.

Crowds gathered to see this masterpiece. The news spread and they came from far and wide to admire that group. There was always a crowd before the chapel, and among the crowd the sculptor was often present.

Once when Michelangelo was there a group of *forestieri* from Lombardy pressed close to the altar, commenting, praising and admiring. One of them asked:

«But who made it?»

«What a question! Il Gobbo of course, our Cristoforo Solari from Milan!», replied one of the Lombards.

That same evening Michelangelo went back to the church. Hidden behind a column he waited for the closing hour, when he would be locked in for the night. He had brought with him a candle and his tools. And the whole night through, with diligent patience, he carved his name on the band lying across the Virgin's breast:

Michael Angelus Bonarotus Florentinus Faciebat.

On the very heart of the Madonna, where all could see it, the solitary artist carved in clear letters his first name, last name and homeland, in a confession that was both painful and triumphant.

Economy and poverty

I N FLORENCE, AFTER Michelangelo's departure, things had gone from bad to worse. Savonarola, defying the orders of the Pope, had begun to preach again, decrying the immorality of the century and the corruption of the Church. Excited by the courage of the friar who dared to oppose the Pope, the people swarmed to hear him. The pulpit in Santa Maria del Fiore was surrounded by crowds of fourteen to fifteen thousand people. «He had at his sermons 15 thousand persons continuously, every working day», states in his diary the shopkeeper Landucci; and adds a little later: «Every time men and women and boys and girls were fainting of hunger».

Black famine reigned in the city. Wheat was not to be found at any price. As if this were not enough, Piero de' Medici was galloping about under the walls, between the Certosa and San Gaggio, at the head of two thousand mercenaries. His brother Giuliano, on the other side of the city, was trying to enroll volunteers.

Then came the first breach, the first protest. A group of young Angry Ones entered the Duomo by night, forcing the door of the bell tower, and covered with a donkey skin and strewed with nails the pulpit where Savonarola was to preach next morning, on Ascension Day. Later the same young ruffians broke up the sermon by loudly banging sticks on the benches reserved for women (the Dominican friar insisted on having women seated on one side, men on the other).

«...And there came from the Pope an excommunication that excommunicated Friar Girolamo».

Now famine was accompanied by epidemic. People were suddenly struck down by fever and died within a few days. «All the heads of households, from 20 to 50 years of age, died, and not the youths and the women».

From Rome the Pope threatened Florence with interdiction. And from Rome the Florentine merchants wrote alarmed letters, afraid of finding themselves boycotted and sacked in retaliation. In Saint Peter's an Augustinian, driven out of Florence, preached before the cardinals, decrying the excommunicated friar and invoking the justice of heaven on the heretical city.

In Florence the protesters grew in number. The Angry Ones were joined by the Compagnacci, who incited the people, famished and impoverished by the epidemic, singling out Francesco Valori as the person responsible for everything.

Added to the protesters in the public square were the scoffers in the convent, the Franciscans of Santa Croce, who preached against Savonarola demonstrating, with the Scriptures at hand, that he was neither a prophet nor God's spokesman, nor that holy man that he pretended to be.

From preaching it was to come to trial, as from words to facts. Florence the city of humanism, cradle and nursery of a genuine reawakening, became, through the fault of two monks, the squalid theater of an anachronistic judgement of God. A Franciscan and a Dominican publicly challenged each other to trial by fire. It was the end of the myth of Savonarola. Legend degenerated into farce. It happened like this.

On April 7, 1498, in Piazza della Signoria, a stake was erected, or more precisely a corridor of wood 50 *braccia* long and 8 wide. At the established hour the opposing factions arrived bearing crosses and banners. The square was packed, but after the preparations nothing happened. Hours passed and the spectators began to murmur. The challengers argued with each other. The Franciscans wanted the Dominican to undress, removing even his underpants, saying that he was «enchanted». The Dominicans demanded that the Franciscan do the same first, showing in public that he was wearing no miraculous talismans or amulets. They went on quarreling till sunset, when the Dominicans decided to go back to the convent, among the whistles and catcalls of the people «who were greatly perturbed, losing faith in the Prophet...».

The Compagnacci took advantage of the situation. The following Sunday, which was Palm Sunday, they assaulted the Convent of San Marco, backed up by those very *fanciugli* who had now turned into bands of snarling curs. They set fire to the door, entered the church, captured Savonarola who was in the choir with the other monks, and, shoving and kicking, drove him to Palazzo della Signoria, where he was imprisoned. On the same night Francesco Valori, the most authoritative supporter of the friar, was killed by the blows of a scythe.

In late April the Pope's pardon reached Florence. On May 23, Girolamo Savonarola, after having confessed under torture everything his enemies desired, was hanged and burned in the square beside his fellow monks Silvestro Maruffi and Domenico da Pescia.

«And as they were hanged all three, Friar Girolamo in the middle, ... they fired the powder and thus burned the structure in an uproar of crackling and flares, and in a few hours they were burned, so that their arms and legs fell off in pieces; and as parts of the bodies remained sticking to the chains, stones were thrown at them to make them fall...».

Michelangelo was in Versilia, quarrying marble for the *Deposition*, when he heard the news of his prophet's death. Perhaps he began the *Pietà* group while caught up in the memory of the preaching he had heard before departing from Florence.

Michelangelo's brothers Buonarroto and Leonardo had already been to see him, unbeknown to each other. Buonarroto spoke to him of their father, in debt to a shopkeeper brother-in-law, Consiglio d'Antonio Cisti, who was threatening to denounce him. At this Michelangelo wrote his father a letter in which the love of a son suddenly burst forth with generous impetuosity. He told his father he had no money, «... but, whatever you ask of me, I will send it to you, even should I be forced to sell myself as a slave!».

Leonardo, fleeing from Viterbo for some unknown reason, undoubtedly persecuted as a fanatical follower of Savonarola, turned to his brother the sculptor for help. «I give notice of how brother Lionardo returned here to Rome, saying that he had had to flee from Viterbo and that they had taken away his cloak...».

Having finished the *Pietà*, Michelangelo sent some of his savings to his father. Meanwhile he kept to himself and the life he led was not a happy one.

At the close of the year 1500 Buonarroto visited him again, reporting to their father that he had found Michelangelo in precarious conditions, as regards both finances and health.

Prudent Lodovico wrote his son a long letter begging him to return, hinting at the possibility of work in Florence. There was, in fact, a block of marble, abandoned in the vicinity of the Church of Santa Maria del Fiore, which the Opera del Duomo had had sent down from the Apuane mountains years ago to be used for the statue of a prophet. That block now bore like wounds the signs of the rough-hewing of Maestro Agostino di Duccio, who had then abandoned the work. Yet in spite of its disfigurement that piece of marble had attracted the attention of three people: Leonardo da Vinci, Andrea Contucci known as Sansovino and the young Michelangelo.

In his letter Lodovico admonished his son, reminding him that, while living economically is good, living in poverty is bad. «Buonarroto tells me that you live there in great economy, or poverty. Economy is good but poverty is bad... and will hurt you in body and soul».

He advised his son not to pinch pennies, because his art required all of his energy, «and should you become ill you would be lost».

Lodovico told Michelangelo the secret of staying healthy, or at least avoiding severe illness: «...and above all take care of your head, keep it moderately warm and never wash yourself; have yourself rubbed but don't wash». Then he gave a never-failing prescription for inflamation of the cheeks, and lastly urged his son to come home, and soon. «I remind you again that you must find a way to come back as soon as you can, and believe me, when you are here you will have enough to do».

This letter is dated December 19, 1500. It would have arrived in Rome after Christmas or in the early new year. Michelangelo did not turn a deaf ear to its appeal.

«Believe me», the laconic Lodovico had written; a sign that he had spoken to someone about his son, to Piero Soderini for instance, one of the most influential men in the government of the new Republic, who may have answered him by saying, «Have him return, and soon. We will have him make beautiful things».

Michelangelo returned to Florence in the Spring. In that same season Soderini was elected Gonfalonier for life.

The slingshot and the bow

JACOPO GALLI DID not want his young friend to return to Florence with empty hands, and saw that he left with the draft of a good contract in his pocket. Michelangelo was commissioned by Archbishop Francesco Todeschini-Piccolomini, the nephew of Pius II and Cardinal of Siena, to sculpt fifteen statues of saints and apostles for the Piccolomini altar in the Duomo of Siena.

As he had for the *Pietà* contract, Jacopo Galli offered himself again as guarantee, promising that the statues «will be the most beautiful that can be seen in modern times». The work was to be completed in three years, for a recompense of five hundred gold ducats, and the sculptor was forbidden to accept any other commission during this time.

The contract contained certain clauses not in keeping with Michelangelo's character, specifying for example that his drawings had to be shown first to the Cardinal for approval, and that the perfection of the statues was to be judged by two masters, one appointed by the client, the other by the sculptor.

One clause in particular seems outright provocative. It seems strange that Michelangelo accepted it; perhaps only due to pressure exerted by Galli, or the need to collect at once the one hundred ducats paid on account, an amount that would solve a number of family problems. The clause obliged the artist to finish a statue of Saint Francis that had been blocked out and then abandoned by no other than Pietro Torrigiani, the hot-tempered companion of the Brancacci Chapel who had broken Michelangelo's nose.

As soon as he returned to Florence Michelangelo started work. He began to rough out four blocks of marble for the first figures: Saint Peter, Saint Paul, Saint Gregory and Saint Pius. But the harder he worked, the more he felt he was regressing.

Those statues all covered in drapery were not suited to a sculptor of nudes like Michelangelo. It was like going back to Bologna, to the time when he had made the angel for the tomb. Rather than creating, he was being forced to imitate.

So he was always ready to put down his chisel and hammer and take a walk. Increasingly often his steps turned in the direction of that enormous block of marble «spoiled» by Master Agostino and abandoned for so many years behind Santa Maria del Fiore.

«He can't take his eyes off it», the Opera del Duomo reported to Soderini. «He goes to see it every day, touches it, measures it, caresses it. What beautiful thing might he make of it?».

But the Gonfalonier had almost decided to give it to Leonardo, now universally famous, who had returned to Florence after the fall of Lodovico il Moro.

«But Michelangelo, Soderini still hasn't said yes, it's not certain. They have spoken to him of you, told him you would make a colossus of it», said Granacci to his friend, «and he doesn't want to disappoint you. Go to see him».

Michelangelo, overcoming his natural reluctance, requested an audience with the Gonfalonier and asked Soderini to give that great block of marble to him. He would make of it, not a statue like the others who wanted it, but a giant. Studying that marble he had realized that he could actually exploit the mistakes of the first rough-hewer, even the holes bored between the legs. And by removing only the indispensable, he would be able to retain the colossal proportions. Moreover, after the trial of the *Pietà*, he felt able to guarantee that the statue would be the most beautiful and the most perfect Florence could ever hope for.

It was a challenge to Leonardo; the younger man pitted against the more famous one. Pier Soderini, concerned and impressed, had the marble assigned to Michelangelo. The conditions were fixed: two years in which to finish the work; six florins a month up to the total amount of four hundred gold florins.

The work was commissioned on August 16th. On September 13, 1501, the artist had already begun to work, after having had a wall built and a stake fence erected in the courtyard of the Opera di Santa Maria del Fiore to keep out curious onlookers.

The limitation set by the Cardinal of Siena, forbidding Michelangelo to accept other commissions for three years, had lasted three months.

He began with drawings, followed by a model made of wax. In one drawing, today in the Louvre, Michelangelo portrayed a David with the head of the giant Goliath at his feet. In the subsequent wax model, David appeared only with his slingshot. The same sheet on which the artist sketched the first version also contains a study of the right arm in the final version. In addition, there are two enigmatic verses that have puzzled scholars over the years:

> *He triumphed with the slingshot*
> *and I with the bow*

> *Michelangelo*

This is an autobiographical confession, as valid at that moment as it was for all of the later events in his long and tormented existence.

The artist is always an unarmed adolescent, struggling against the conventions, the habits and the vices of a society that is as powerful in structure and as tough as a giant. The sculptor stands alone, armed with the slingshot of his courage, before the dense, unfeeling material. Genius is always alone, armed only by its faith, pitted against the giant that represents the conformity of the age. David vanquished Goliath with a slingshot; I, Michelangelo, with a bow. Perhaps this is an allusion to the tools used for the first rough-hewing of the stone, perhaps not. What matters is not a technical detail, but the human and spiritual affinity, the inner similitude.

Two years of cloistered retreat in the courtyard of the Opera del Duomo passed, with no news filtering to the world outside. Although Michelangelo revealed nothing it can be guessed that he worked incessantly on his giant, at least in the first three months; day and night, without rest, without a pause, to delete all the chisel marks left by Master Agostino, especially in places where so little marble remained that he could only smooth and polish.

Like a dark insect buzzing around an immense plant, up and down on the scaffolding, his homely face beside the magnificent features that were emerging from nothing, by daylight and by candlelight, his hair turned gray by the marble dust, as if nourishing his creation with his very breath, Michelangelo lived and consummated in solitude, to the end, the conception and birth of his masterpiece.

On January 25, 1504, the work was finished.

In the meantime Alexander VI had died and the Cardinal of Siena had been elected Pope under the name of Pius III. Michelangelo trembled. The new Pope would demand immediately that he account for the fifteen statues commissioned for the Duomo of Siena. But after only 27 days as pope, Pius III died, leaving a will that enjoined his heirs, Jacopo and Andrea Piccolomini, to have the statues completed for the altar.

Totally absorbed in the David, Michelangelo was late with the consignments. He had finished the first four figures, assisted by Baccio da Montelupo, but had not even started the others. He was granted an extension. The contract was amended because the Florentines, at war with Pisa, were trying to deviate the course of the Arno to isolate the enemy city, and the river barges transporting the marble could no longer reach Florence. But these were only excuses. For Michelangelo those works belonged to the past, and he wished to hear no more of them. Out of the money he had received on account he owed one hundred ducats, and this gave rise to a «tragedy of the altar» that was to conclude only sixty years later when, aged and remorseful, he asked for and was given full absolution from any commitment. It was another Archbishop of Siena, another Piccolomini, who granted his request.

The giant in the square

WHAT WOULD HAPPEN today if the Mayor of Florence, instead of convening the municipal council, called a committee of experts to decide where a statue by Michelangelo should be placed?

Piero Soderini did not convene the «great» Council, with over one thousand members, nor the «small» one made up of eighty men, but appointed a committee of artists and citizens interested in art to examine Michelangelo's *David* and express an opinion on both the quality of the work and the best place for it.

The young Buonarroti must have trembled, for those experts were:

Andrea della Robbia
Benedetto Buglioni
Giovanni delle Corniole

Attavante, illuminator
Messer Francesco, Herald of the Signoria
Monciatto, woodworker (or inlayer)
Giovanni Cellini, piper (father of Benvenuto)
Lorenzo della Volpaia
Bonaccorso di Bartoluccio (nephew of Lorenzo Ghiberti)
Salvastro, jeweler
Michelagnolo, goldsmith (father of Baccio Bandinelli)
Cosimo Rosselli
Gaspare di Simone, goldsmith (father of Bernardo Baldi-
ni known as Bernardino)
Lodovico, goldsmith and foundry master (father of the
sculptor Lorenzo Lotti, known as Lorenzetto)
Andrea known as Riccio, goldsmith
Gallieno, embroiderer
David del Ghirlandaio
Simone del Pollaiolo known as Cronaca
Filippino Lippi
Sandro Botticelli
Giuliano and Antonio da Sangallo
Andrea del Monte a Sansovino
Chimenti del Tasso
Francesco Granacci
Biagio Tucci
Bernardo della Cecca, woodworker and architect
Piero di Cosimo
Leonardo da Vinci
Pietro Perugino.

As to the excellence of the work they all concurred. Rival-
ry and jealousy had to yield to admiration. Knowing all
about the spoiled block of marble, the committee unani-
mously declared that Michelangelo had overcome difficul-

ties thought to be insuperable, and in creating such a beautiful statue had worked a greater miracle than if he had brought a dead man back to life.

As to where the statue should be placed, opinions differed. Some wanted it under Orcagna's loggia, others on the terrace before the Palace of the Signoria in place of Donatello's Judith. This was in fact to be the final choice, approved by the sculptor.

The small Council, having heard the decision of the experts, commissioned the architects Giuliano and Antonio da Sangallo, assisted by the two «woodworkers» Baccio d'Agnolo and Bernardo della Cecca, to transport the giant to the square.

In the words of a chronicler, «On the 14th day of May, 1504, the marble giant was pulled from the Opera. It issued forth at the hour of 24, and they broke the wall above the door to let it out, and in the night there were thrown certain stones at the giant to damage it. They had to mount guard that night, and they went very slowly, with the statue bound so straight, with very strong boards and with great ingenuity, that when it swayed its feet did not touch the ground. It struggled 4 days to arrive in the square, arriving there on the 18th at the hour of 12. There were more than 40 men to make it go. It had under it 14 boards joined together, which changed from hand to hand; and they struggled until the 8th day of June 1504 to place it above the railing where had been the Judith, which they took down and put in the palace...».

At last the statue was raised on its base and Michelangelo could start to give it the finishing touches.

This twenty-nine-year-old sculptor was small in stature, bow-legged, with a big head on a fragile body, a nose crushed like a prize-fighter's, curly black hair, tangled and «never washed» according to the advice of Messer Lodovico, a dark beard, big, strong hands with the wide-spread fingers that knew how to shape marble so skillfully, now grasping the heavy chisel, now the most delicate of tools.

Up and down a ladder he went, all around his colossus, touching, smoothing, polishing, cleaning; observing through half-closed eyes, contemplating, judging and correcting.

One morning Soderini, leaving the Palace and stopping to look up at the statue from below, called out:

«Oh Michelangelo, it looks to me like the nose is too big».

The sculptor realized at once that the Gonfalonier had stopped at the wrong point, right under the figure, where the perspective was falsified, but he said nothing. Picking up a handful of dust, he climbed up the ladder to the head of the colossus. Pretending to chisel, he let some dust and marble chips drop onto Soderini's head, obliging him to move backward a few steps.

«Magnificent Messer», asked Michelangelo a few moments later, «and now how does it look to you?»

«I like it better now. You've put life back into him».

And alive the statue was to remain, through the centuries, this marvel of human genius that evoked the cry of «miracle», drawing artists and merchants, churchmen and soldiers, the nobility and the populace, from all over Italy to look at it.

«This work has surpassed all statutes, modern and ancient, Greek and Latin», was to exclaim Vasari later, «and he who sees it need not bother to see other works of sculpture done in our times or in others by any other artificer».

Two holes bored in the pupils to accentuate, in the play of light, the intensity of the expression; the head held proud and high; an attitude of composure, but with every nerve and muscle ready to leap into action; the self-assurance of a strong, pure man facing his enemy – David is all this, and more. He is the image of an inner reality common to all men, since in each of us lies hidden a David, just as there is always, lying in wait, a Goliath.

> *David with the slingshot*
> *and I with the bow.*

A stingy friend

T HE DUKE OF Rohan, Marshall of Gié and favorite of Louis XII King of France, had hinted to the Signoria of Florence that he would like to have a David like that of Donatello, which he had probably seen in 1494 while in the retinue of Charles VIII. Soderini, for obvious political reasons, hoping to secure the alliance of France against Pisa, waited for Michelangelo to finish the marble giant. Then he summoned the sculptor to commission of him another David, this time in bronze, no more than two and a quarter *braccia* in height.

Michelangelo remembered one of his first drawings for the colossus in the square, the one with the verse on the slingshot and the bow, where David was represented with the head of Goliath at his feet. He proposed a figure inspired by that drawing to the Signoria, and on August 12, 1504, the statue was officially commissioned of him.

Now Michelangelo was like Briareus of the hundred arms. It was not enough, this second David, nor his renewed commitment with the heirs of Pius III for the statues ordered for the Piccolomini altar in Siena. He also agreed to make, for two Flemish merchants (Giovanni and Alessandro Mouscron) a Madonna with Child, which came to be known as the *Bruges* Madonna; for the Florentine Taddeo Taddei a marble tondo representing the Madonna with Child and the infant Saint

John; for another Florentine, Bartolommeo Pitti, another marble tondo with another Madonna and Child; and from the Wool Merchant's Guild he accepted a commission to sculpt twelve marble statues, each representing an apostle, for the church of Santa Maria del Fiore.

To relax between one statue and another he began to paint a tondo for his friend Agnolo Doni.

In Michelangelo's long life there were frequent times of total identification of the man with his work; first the David, now this group of works that would have taken anyone a lifetime to complete; and soon the vault of the Sistine Chapel, no longer the work of a man but of a titan, then the Medici chapels, and again the Sistine with that Last Judgement that would seem to demand not one, but many lifetimes.

If the beauty of Michelangelo's work has, for centuries, been breathtaking to those who view it for the first or the hundredth time, the sheer bulk of it, measured in time and space, is not just amazing but awesome. For this reason all of Michelangelo's biographers and commentators have employed adjectives and superlatives that seem prodigiously exaggerated and rhetorical; seem so, but are not. They are attempts to define the indefinable, since Michelangelo was truly, when measured by our standards, a titan, a superhuman prodigy. By his own standards, instead, he was only a passionate seeker after beauty and truth, a man always defeated by his own greatness.

To return to the statues, the second David was modeled in clay and then cast in bronze. The artist was assisted in the casting by Benedetto da Rovezzo, a master foundryman.

The statue was not yet finished when the Duke of Rohan began to fall into disgrace. Soderini, for the usual reasons of state, was now turning a deaf ear to the insistent requests of the Duke transmitted through his ambassadors. When the downfall of the Duke and Marshall was certain, the Signoria informed him that the statue would remain in Florence.

«Fine friends these Florentines are», indignantly exclaimed the new favorite of the King of France, the Minister of Finance Florimondo Robertet. «They had made a David for the Duke of Rohan and seeing that he has fallen from the grace of our Majesty, they have refused to send it to him!».

But the Florentine ambassadors soon appeased Robertet by convincing the Signoria to give the David to him instead. So in 1508 Michelangelo's bronze was embarked at Ponte a Signa, and down the Arno, then by sea, it sailed to France. Robertet, thanking the Florentine Republic for this precious and greatly appreciated gift, and reconfirming his sovereign's friendship in the dispute with Pisa, took the statue to his Castle of Bury, from where it was later transferred to the Castle of Villeroy. From that time on all trace of it has been lost.

But the *Bruges Madonna*, one of Michelangelo's most beautiful and mysterious Madonnas, has not been lost.

The distant gaze, as if fixed in a void, is that of a mother who foresees the tragic fate of her son. The composure of the person, the fixed expression of the face, isolate her in indescribable melancholy, while the Child standing at her knees, with his round curly head and severe, almost frowning expression, bends slightly toward her, taking her hand in a loving gesture that only emphasizes his mother's suffering.

The tondo executed for Taddeo Taddei slightly later is the first in that series of works called unfinished by some critics. It was instead the artist's precise intention to leave them like this, between finished and unfinished, to heighten the plastic emphasis of the main figures.

This marble tondo is now in the Royal Academy of Fine Arts in London. The face and the drapery of the Madonna, and the body of the Child down to the knees, are finished and polished, while the signs of the chisel can be seen in the Virgin's hair and her son's legs, and still more in the infant Saint John. The figures are brought into higher relief by the chiaroscuro effect, emerging from the dull, dense marble into the clear light. They seem to illustrate in stone the neo-platonic words of the humanists:

«...I believe that painting may be considered better the more it approaches relief, and relief may be considered worse the more it approaches painting... I consider sculpture to be work which is done by taking away. What is done by adding is similar to painting...», Michelangelo was to write years later to Benedetto Varchi.

The tondo for Bartolommeo Pitti, later given to Francesco Guicciardini and now in the Bargello Museum in Florence, confirms this principle once again.

The marks of the chisel and rough gradine are everywhere, except on the face and in the drapery of the Madonna. The infant Saint John is barely roughed out in the marble. The Virgin does not have the mournful expression of the Bruges Madonna. She is a woman with a beautiful, proud head, seated in regal majesty. From hip to knee her legs are very long, and short from knee to ankle. If she rose to her feet she would be out of proportion, almost deformed.

Such innovative foreshortening was to abound, a few years later, in the vault of the Sistine Chapel.

«Michelangelo, you must paint me a Holy Family, as a gift to Maddalena Strozzi when she becomes my wife».

«Agnolo, I'm sorry, but I can't do it. Don't you see how busy I am? All these marbles to finish...».

«Michelangelo, for the sake of our friendship, do me this favor. You could make a round painting like these marbles. A beautiful Madonna with Joseph and the Child».

«I'll have to think about it».

He did not stop to think for long. In the pauses between one blow of the chisel and another, the canvas on its easel began to fill with images: a Madonna in the center, seated on the ground, turning to receive from Joseph standing behind her the curly-headed child. The chiaroscuro of the drapery and the muscles, accentuated more than is usual in painting, puts the figures in sculptural relief. Behind them in the background a bizarre group of nudes seated on a wall seems a parade of adolescents from pagan times, depicted in an attitude of joyous and sublime indifference.

When he had finished the painting and mounted it in a sumptuous gilded frame of his own design, Michelangelo sent it to his friend Agnolo Doni.

«Consign it to him alone», he cautioned his assistant, «and have him give you seventy ducats».

«Beautiful! Magnificent», exclaimed Doni when he saw the painting. But then the merchant's stinginess prevailed over friendship and enthusiasm, and counting out the coins he gave the boy forty ducats.

«Tell Michelangelo that forty are enough».

«Go back at once», Michelangelo told his assistant. «Go to Agnolo Doni's house and tell them to give you either the painting or one hundred ducats».

Doni, who had called his friends in to admire the painting, had no intention of sending it back. He went to find another thirty ducats and gave it to the young man.

«Go back!», cried Michelangelo to the frightened boy, «Go and take back the picture. If Doni wants to keep it, tell him it now costs one hundred and forty ducats!»

The Florentine merchant preferred to keep the painting; and with a sigh he paid the difference, double what the artist had asked of him before his imprudent attempt to get a discount.

The great challenge

SODERINI, IN THE meantime, had had an extraordinary idea. He had asked Leonardo da Vinci to fresco a battle scene on one of the long walls in the Hall of the Great Council (now called the Hall of the Five Hundred). Slightly later he assigned Michelangelo the opposite wall to decorate with the same theme.

We can only imagine what that hall would be like today if the two artists had been able to carry out their commissions. It would be the most amazingly beautiful room in the world.

Leonardo had chosen as subject the battle of Anghiari, and had been given a room in Santa Maria Novella to prepare the cartoons. Michelangelo chose an episode from the battle of Cascina, and had a room in Sant'Onofrio to work on the cartoons.

The great challenge had been hurled.

Leonardo da Vinci was then at the height of his fame. He had already completed, for the monks of San Domenico in Milan, that Last Supper in Santa Maria delle Grazie which had been described as the highest expression of all his studies and writings. In Milan he had also designed and modeled an equestrian statue of Francesco Sforza, of such size that 200,000 pounds of bronze would be needed for its casting. «Seeking always excellence above excellence, and perfection above perfection», Leonardo did not want to cast it in several pieces but all entire, and had wasted time searching for new casting techniques. In the meantime the Duchy of Milan had fallen into the hands of the French, and the prodigious model of the statue had been destroyed by Gascon crossbowmen.

In Florence, «a city avid of speaking and which judges things by their success and not by hearsay», as Machiavelli noted about that time, the news spread in the form of malicious rumor. It was said that Leonardo had made a colossal model, but had been unable to cast it in bronze.

«Attractive of person was Lionardo, well-proportioned, graceful and of goodly countenance. He wore a rose-hued garment short to the knee, when long jerkins were the fashion. He had thick hair down to the middle of his chest and he went adorned with rings and well composed».

Handsome and extravagant, well-dressed and refined: the opposite of Michelangelo, ugly, shabby and neglected. Leonardo was fifty-two years old, Michelangelo twenty-nine.

Although with some diffidence that may have been tinged with jealousy, Leonardo admired the young sculptor, recognizing his exceptional talent. Michelangelo, on the contrary, was openly jealous of Leonardo, not through envy, but through natural, instinctive emulation. He could feel second to no one. With the *David* he had provoked Leonardo and now he was challenging him on his own terrain as painter with the cartoons for the battle. Leonardo had imagined a scene of horsemen rushing into the fray around a banner. Michelangelo had chosen a pause in the battle, a moment when the Florentine soldiers, while bathing in the Arno, were surprised by trumpets of alarm announcing the enemy.

All Florence reveled in the spectacle. If Leonardo's cartoons showed unrivaled skill in drawing and composition, those of Michelangelo were on a comparable level. The former showed a harmonious balance of horses and riders in the tangled confusion of battle; the latter the anatomy of nude bodies, so vividly alive in the convulsive motions of surprise that they seemed about to leap from the drawing.

No one took sides for one or the other. In profound respect the people of Florence watched, fully aware of the birth of two masterpieces that would testify over the centuries to the genius and the glory of the times.

Michelangelo, increasingly surly and withdrawn, knew perfectly well that he was not competing with a Granacci or a Torrigiani, but with an artist that even kings addressed with deferential respect. And since he could not mock him, one day he insulted him. An anonymous biographer of Leonardo relates that the painter, passing one day with a friend in front of Santa Trinita, where many «worthy men» were discussing a passage from Dante, was stopped and asked to give his interpretation. At that moment Michelangelo happened by and Leonardo, seeing him, said:

«Ask it of him, for he will tell you much better than I can».

Michelangelo, wrongly feeling himself ridiculed, angrily replied, «Tell them yourself, that you made a horse to cast in bronze and you could not cast it and for shame you abandoned it!», and strode away in a fury.

Leonardo had not spoken to mock him, but because Michelangelo's profound knowledge of Dante was well-known. He blushed with indignation and walked away with his friend in silence.

Here again is a Michelangelo who is hard to define, not merely surly but rude and insulting. Jealousy had overcome him. At the sight of Leonardo he had lost control of himself, replying to an outstretched hand with a bite.

Then, all at once, he broke down. Having completed the Madonnas, roughed out the figure of an apostle, painted the Doni tondo, and prepared the cartoons for the battle of Cascina, he suddenly felt he had asked too much of himself. The wear and tear of the immense effort that, from the start of the David, had continued unbroken up that day, was beginning to tell. Today it would be called a nervous breakdown. But instead of taking a vacation or dosing himself with medicine, Michelangelo took refuge in poetry and cured himself with verses.

He was thirty years old. Love, though still without a name, was knocking at his door. He was in love with love, and Petrarch was the master who guided his hand in those first literary efforts.

«Michelangelo, may I come in?»

«Look who's here, it's Sangallo! Where do you come from?»

«From Rome».

«And what news have you brought?»

«One thing only, but important. The Pope is calling for you».

With these words Giuliano da Sangallo pulled out a purse filled with one hundred ducats and threw it on the table.

«His Holiness has sent you this. Michelangelo», added the architect, «this is a Pope who wants to do great things, and says he has already waited too many years. Bramante is working for him, and so am I. Now he needs you. What should I tell him?».

Michelangelo felt that that call, like the encounter with Lorenzo the Magnificent in the sculpture garden of San Marco, marked another appointment with destiny, to be accepted without hesitation.

«Don't tell him anything», he answered. «I'm coming with you».

PART TWO

Megalomania

G IULIANO DELLA ROVERE, the nephew of Pope Sixtus IV, elected cardinal at the age of twenty-eight in 1471, had hoped to rise soon to the throne of Saint Peter. Instead, Innocent VIII, Alexander VI and Pius III were elected before him. After almost twenty years of waiting, upon the death of the Piccolomini Pope his turn came at last.

The new pope had to make up for lost time, to leave to posterity a lasting memorial of his papacy.

Bramante was immediately taken into his service, followed by Giuliano da Sangallo. Then came the turn of Michelangelo, and lastly that of Raphael, a distant relative of Bramante.

«Here, Holy Father, this is the project you asked me for».

Julius II took the rolled-up drawing from Michelangelo's hand and spread it open to examine it. It was a project for his tomb. He had called to Rome the greatest sculptor of the age to make for him, in the Basilica of Saint Peter's, a funeral monument. Like the pharaohs with their pyramids and the emperors with their mausoleums, this warrior pope who had decided to unify Italy wanted a tomb that had no equal.

It was not yet a month since Michelangelo had arrived in Rome and the Pope had spoken to him of the monument, and already the project, clear in every detail, was ready. The megalomania of Julius II had met its match in the giganto-mania of Michelangelo.

The artist had designed an enormous parallelepiped, its four faces standing free, with the base corresponding to one and a half squares. All around the base were niches holding statues. Between the niches were pillars to which other figures were bound «like captives». Above the niches and the pillars ran a cornice that framed the whole monument, on which rested four great statues, among them that of Moses. Above those, on another storey, two angels held up an arch. Under the arch lay the tomb.

There were forty marble statues, in addition to the bronze bas-reliefs narrating the life of the Pope; a multitude of figures and symbols, a whole world gathered around a corpse.

Julius II, openly showing his satisfaction, immediately sent for Bramante and Sangallo.

«Where shall we put this tomb?».

It was on that day, and to make a place for that monument, that the Pope decided to rebuild the Basilica of Saint Peter's.

Visiting the church with Michelangelo and the two architects he tried to find a worthy place, but space was lacking. At that time the church was in the form of a cross. At its head Pope Nicolas V had started to build a new tribune, but it had remained at a height of three *braccia*. The walls would have to be raised and a roof built.

«How much would it cost?», demanded Julius II.

«At least one hundred thousand *scudi*», answered Michelangelo.

«Let it be two hundred thousand instead», replied the Pope, «but let the whole basilica be rebuilt».

Bramante was commissioned to study a project and present it as soon as possible. Michelangelo was ordered to go to Carrara to select marble for the tomb and have it quarried.

So it was due to Michelangelo, for better or worse, that the new temple of Saint Peter's came into being. The church that had stood up to then dated from the time of Constantine. Many emperors, starting with Charlemagne, had been crowned there, many saints had been raised to glory, and all of the popes, with rare exceptions, had received their supreme consecration.

But Bramante had not turned deaf ears to the Pope's request. His project respected neither the ancient structure nor the old plan. Columns and vaults, walls and facades, all were to be torn down and rebuilt.

«This is not a Bramante, but a *ruinante*», murmured the scandalized dignitaries and monsignors of the Curia.

The square in front of the church had become a worksite, bristling with piles, thick with scaffolding, thronged with masons and builders, swarming with caravans of oxen and donkeys, loading and unloading their carts even by torch light.

Meanwhile Michelangelo had taken the road back to Florence, where Alamanno Salviati paid out to him, on behalf of the Pope, a thousand ducats. With that amount he traveled on to Carrara, where he stayed for eight months.

The artist camped out beside the miners, the stonemasons, the mule drivers and carters. He was up at dawn inspecting the quarries, sampling the marble for quality and color, watching the great blocks as they rumbled heavily down the mountain, measuring them, having them cut in slabs. Then he roughed out the statues with great blows of the hammer and chisel, discerning in each block the figure that lay sleeping within, and sent them down to the sea to be loaded on barges that sailed along the coast down to Ostia, then up the Tiber to Rome.

And he observed. The Apuane mountains, tinged with pink and purple at dawn and sunset, spoke to his imagination. One day, looking up from the seacoast at one of those mountains, Michelangelo thought of sculpting in it a gigantic figure which «would appear to sailors from afar».

There too it would be enough to remove the superfluous, and the mountain of marble would be transformed into a colossus. But Autumn, bringing the first fogs and rains, left him no time to begin. He had to return to Rome, anxious to start work on the tomb but with grief in his heart for the giant who was not to be.

From the windows of his palace the Pope observed the blocks of marble that were accumulating in the square, which gave «to others admiration and to him gladness». As soon as Michelangelo returned he began to plan with him every detail, making frequent visits to the artist's studio.

To supervise the work even better Julius II had a gangway constructed that led from the corridor of the papal palace directly to Michelangelo's studio.

Jealousy and superstition

THIS FRATERNAL COMPANIONSHIP between pope and artist was not, however, to last long. Julius' affection for Michelangelo triggered the envy of all about him, and of Bramante in particular. Knowing how greatly the Pope esteemed Michelangelo, Bramante began to insinuate doubts, not so about much the artist as about the tomb itself.

«It's unlucky, Holy Father. It's for good reason that the people, whose proverbs are always right, say that it brings bad luck to build your tomb while still alive. We don't want Your Holiness to run the risk of having to use it before its time.

Michelangelo is a very great artist and Your Holiness must keep him with you. Why not have him work at painting?».

One such suggestion today, another tomorrow, and superstition won out, in the end, over logic. The Pope's enthusiasm began to cool.

Michelangelo realized this, but did not dare to speak, or perhaps preferred not to.

He continued to work on the figures of the prisoners, while the white blocks of marble from the Apuane mountains went on traveling up the Tiber.

On the day when the last barge was unloaded Michelangelo went as usual to the Pope to get money to pay the transport charges. But he found the antechamber packed, and the Pope sent word to him to come back later. He paid the boatsmen out of his own pocket, so they would not have to wait before returning to Carrara, deciding to go to the Pope another day. When it seemed the right moment, he presented himself at the antechamber of Julius II, but was not received. He tried again the next day, with the same results. On the following day he returned, insisting that the Pope receive him.

«Pardon me, Messer», one of the footmen told him, «but I have had orders not to let you enter».

A bishop who happened to be present admonished the footman:

«You must not know this man, or you wouldn't speak to him like that!».

«On the contrary, Monsignor, I know him well; but unfortunately I have had these orders and I must follow them».

«You can tell the Pope», cried Michelangelo indignantly, «that if he wants to see me from now on, he will have to come and look for me!». And he stalked out slamming the door behind him.

Upon arriving home he ordered his two assistants to sell all the furniture and meet him in Florence. Then by post, never pausing at an inn but changing horses at every stop, he arrived at Poggibonsi, a castle of defense for the Florentine Republic, at two o'clock in the morning. There, feeling safe at last, he rested.

The couriers of Julius II were not long in arriving. Michelangelo had just arisen from his brief rest after the flight when five horsemen entered the inn searching for him.

«Is Messer Michelangelo, the Florentine sculptor, here?»

«Yes, he arrived last night», replied the innkeeper.

«Call him», ordered the one who seemed to be in charge.

And when Michelangelo appeared: «Messer», he said, «I have an order to take you back to Rome».

«I'm not going», replied Michelangelo. «I am a citizen of Florence and here we are in the territory of the Republic».

The innkeeper, hearing the name of Michelangelo, had remembered the colossus in the square, which he too had made a special trip to see, and had called his helpers. Arriving with menacing scowls, one armed with skewers, another with springs and shovels, they formed a circle around the Pope's messengers.

«I appeal to these my fellow citizens», continued Michelangelo. «The Pope's guards are not allowed to arrest a Florentine citizen in the territory of Florence. And if you dare to touch me ...».

The five guards looked around them. The faces of the onlookers were threatening.

«No, no, Messer Michelangelo, we don't want to arrest you. We have orders to find you and take you back to His Holiness. But since you have crossed the boundary, we have no authority over you. We ask only one thing of you. Read this letter from the Holy Father and answer as you think best, but specifying the place where we found you».

Michelangelo read the letter in which the Pope enjoined him «having read this, return at once to Rome, under penalty of disgrace».

Calling for paper, pen and ink, Michelangelo replied that «... he had no intention of ever returning; and that in exchange for good and faithful service he did not deserve this, that is, to have been expelled from the Pope's sight like an evildoer; and since His Holiness did not wish to continue with the tomb, he felt no further obligation, and did not want to commit himself to anything else». He added the date, from Poggibonsi, and his signature.

The couriers took the road back to Rome.

Having eaten and drunk, and finally free from fear, Michelangelo thanked the innkeeper and started off for Florence by the next post carriage.

The Pope's briefs

«MICHELANGELO, I HAVE a brief from the Pope in which he asks the Republic of Florence to have you return to Rome immediately», said Pier Soderini, waving aloft a sheet of paper.

«But I'm not going back», replied Michelangelo.

«Stay here then», returned the Gonfalonier. «You still have to finish the fresco of the battle and the wall is there waiting for you. The Opera del Duomo has also told me that you still have to complete the Saint Matthew and begin the other eleven apostles. The Pope has problems right now, with the Baglioni of Perugia and the Bentivoglio of Bologna. He'll forget all about you before long».

It is highly probable that Machiavelli, who played a leading part in the complicated diplomacy of Florence, was also present during this conversation. Although no record of this remains, the documents of the time clearly show that the sculptor and the Secretary of the Republic were well acquainted and frequently in contact.

So the government of the Signoria was on Michelangelo's side, and he set to work at once. First, however, he had to explain his reasons to the Pope in more detail than in the note written at Poggibonsi. Two weeks after his sudden flight, he wrote to his friend Giuliano da Sangallo:

«Giuliano, I have heard how displeased the Pope was at my departure... but it is true that on Holy Saturday I heard the Pope say, when speaking with a jeweler at table, that he had no intention of spending one bit more, neither for small stones nor for large ones; ... and again, before I left, I asked him part of what was owed me to continue with the work. His Holiness answered that I should come back Monday, and I did come back on Monday, and Tuesday, and Wednesday, and Thursday; ... on the last day, Friday morning, I was sent out, that is driven away. Now you are writing me on behalf of the Pope, and so read this to the Pope...».

The Pope, however, refused to give up. After the first brief, which had no effect, he sent another more emphatic one to which Soderini was forced to reply, saying that Michelangelo was very much afraid; that before he could return, he would have to be reassured as to His Holiness' intentions and that «if you don't go gently, he will go away from here as he has already wanted to do twice».

Michelangelo, in the meanwhile, was working on his cartoons, brooding over the insult, talking to himself as if he were in the Pope's presence, even writing him a sonnet in which, among other things, he admonished him in heartfelt tones:

You believed in lying words
and rewarded he who is the real enemy.

In the Council Hall, Leonardo had begun to paint the wall with disastrous results. Instead of frescoing it he had decided to use oil paints, and the color, not drying as fast as it should, dripped down the wall destroying every image.

It was probably at this time that Michelangelo, exasperated by the incident with the Pope, had a violent argument with Perugino, so violent that the latter had him summoned «before the Magistrate of the Eight», or, as we would say today, denounced him for abusive insults.

Pietro Vannucci, known as Perugino, was at the time the official painter of Florence. «For money», wrote Vasari, «he would have done any evil».

Instead of doing evil, he painted for whoever paid him best. His style had become the rage, and priests and monks fought to have him paint sumptuously adorned Madonnas and elegant, well-dressed saints to adorn their altars.

Having heard wonders of Michelangelo's cartoons, Perugino wanted to see them for himself. His reaction to that «scandalous» exhibition of nude bodies can be easily imagined. It was the protest of the academic hack against the innovations of a man of genius. His comments, increasingly biting, were repeated to Michelangelo who, meeting him one day surrounded by people, rudely grasped him by the collar, shouting that his art was «crude».

Humiliated in his dignity and prestige, Perugino denounced him. But the «Eight» (or Pier Soderini?) acquitted Michelangelo, and Pietro Vannucci «was left with very little honor».

Now a third and more threatening brief from Julius II seriously alarmed the government of Florence.

«Michelangelo», the worried Gonfalonier told him, «you can't keep on defying the Pope. You have already tried him as not even the King of France would dare. Now don't make him ask you again, prepare to leave!».

«I'm not leaving».

«You will leave, Michelangelo! We don't want a war because of you. We can't let our Republic run this risk».

«I'll go to Turkey then, to the Sultan who has sent to call me», replied Michelangelo.

«No, you will go to the Pope. A Christian like you cannot do otherwise. Better to die going to the Pope than to live going to the Turk. However», Soderini reassured him, «the Pope is kindly disposed toward you; and if you are still afraid, the Signoria of Florence will send you with an ambassador's credentials».

Michelangelo, resigned but not reassured, prepared to leave. It was early September of 1506, and the Pope had already marched out of Rome at the head of his troops to wage war on Perugia. Niccolò Machiavelli was on a mission with Julius II, and a letter addressed to him from Biagio Bonaccorsi, a member of the Council of the Ten of War, announced that he had sent him some money «by Michelagnolo the sculptor». But in a second letter Bonaccorsi wrote to Machiavelli: «When I believed that Michelagnolo had given you that money, it was brought back to me by one of his men, who told me that it had been sent back for good reason».

For what reason? We do not know. But now Soderini was really nervous. The Pope had been informed that Michelangelo was arriving, and he would never have tolerated being deceived.

Probably the Gonfalonier and Michelangelo were merely waiting for the right moment. The Pope in fact, having taken Perugia, headed straight for Bologna, making a triumphal entry on November 11th after Giovanni Bentivoglio had fled the city.

With safe-conducts from a Cardinal and from Soderini, Michelangelo started off for Bologna. The Gonfalonier had also given him a letter formally addressed to his brother Cardinal Soderini, but in reality meant for the Pope.

«We certify Your Signoria that he is a good young man and in his art unique in Italy, perhaps in the universe. We can more precisely recommend him: his character is such that for gentle words and caresses, he will do anything. You must show him love and do him favors and he will make things to cause those who see them to marvel...».

The Gonfalonier of Florence was taking preventive action to ward off any negative reaction from Julius II.

Toward the end of November Michelangelo arrived at Bologna. Before presenting himself to the Pope he went to Saint Petronius to hear mass; but in church were some footmen from the papal court who recognized him and convinced him to follow them at once to the palace of the Sixteen. Julius II was at table with a group of cardinals, but the footmen, knowing the Pope's desire to have Michelangelo back again, announced him anyway and brought him into the room. The sculptor, suddenly finding himself face to face with the terrible old man, knelt at a respectful distance.

«You were supposed to come to us, and you have waited for us to come to you», said Julius II with a frown.

«Holy Father, I ask pardon. I did not do it out of ill will nor to offend you, but because I could not bear to be driven from your home like that».

Grim and silent, the Pope stared at the kneeling artist.

«Your Holiness, don't hold his mistake against him», intervened Cardinal Soderini, «he erred through ignorance. Artists, apart from their art, are all like this».

«You insult him!», cried the Pope. «You are offending him more than we have done! It's you who are ignorant, wretch, and not him! Get out of my sight, go to the devil!».

And since the poor Cardinal was too shocked to move, the Pope ordered his servants to throw him out.

Having vented his rage, Julius II told Michelangelo to approach, pardoned him, blessed him, told him to rise and ordered him to stay in Bologna and await his next instructions.

The breviary and the sword

«IMPETUS AND AUDACITY often obtain what could never be gotten with ordinary manners». These words of Machiavelli summarized in a single phrase the whole policy of Julius II. Before the Concistory convened in August 1506, he had solemnly declared his intention of «cleaning out the tyrants» from the Papal States, with the aid of the King of France and the Florentines.

Piero Soderini, rightly concerned at the Pope's announcement and reluctant to make an enemy of Bentivoglio, lord of Bologna and friend of Louis XII King of France, sent Machiavelli to meet the Pope who had marched out of Rome with an imposing retinue of courtiers and soldiers.

At Civita Castellana the Secretary of the Republic of Florence had his first audience with the warrior Pope, informing him of the fears of the Signoria: first, that the support of the French was not certain; second, that the Pope was not truly convinced of that undertaking; third, that His Holiness might end up by coming to terms with Bentivoglio without expelling him from Bologna.

Julius II replied to the first doubt by showing a letter from Louis XII exhorting him to carry out this initiative and assuring him of his aid; to the second by saying that he could show his conviction no better than by going in person, as he was in fact doing; to the third that Bentivoglio would have to be crazy to stay in Bologna.

Machiavelli, having reassured the council of the Ten of War, remained with the Pope's army, ready to intercede when necessary.

Reaching Orvieto, the Pope met with his first success. Giampaolo Baglioni, Lord of Perugia, came out to meet him, formally subjugating himself and putting himself in the hands of the Pope. From Perugia the Pope marched on to Cesena. Having finally received confirmation that the King of France was sending him, from Milan, the promised aid, he traversed Florentine territory, purposely avoiding that of Venice in respect for its neutrality, and reached Imola on October 26th. Giovanni Bentivoglio, seeing himself abandoned by his powerful French ally, fled the city, and on November 11th the Pope entered Bologna.

Some two weeks later, without any advance notice, Michelangelo arrived.

«Now you will make me a great bronze statue. How much do you think it will cost?»

«Holy Father, I am not experienced in casting because it is not my art; maybe a thousand ducats or more, but I can't commit myself to the amount until I have cast the statue».

Two months later the clay model was ready. The Pope went often to watch his friend work, conversing cheerfully with him, and the artist took advantage of these visits to have him pose.

«Holiness, what do you want me to put in your left hand, a breviary?»

«Not a breviary, Michelangelo. A sword! But that right hand, so vigorous», added the Pope with a smile, «what is it doing? Blessing or cursing?»

«Warning, Holy Father, warning this people to be prudent».

The statue of Julius II was about seven *braccia* high, three times life size. It portrayed the Pope seated, his right hand raised, and was to be placed in a niche on the facade of San Petronio.

Michelangelo, inexperienced in casting, had called for two assistants from Florence: Lapo and Lodovico. Lapo was a Florentine sculptor regularly employed by the Opera del Duomo. Lodovico Lotti, the father of the sculptor Lorenzetto, had been a goldsmith's apprentice in the studio of Antonio del Pollaiolo, and then a master foundryman for the artillery of the Florentine Republic. He had also been a member of the committee of experts appointed to decide on a place for the *David*.

It is hard to imagine today the life Michelangelo led in Bologna, camped out in a rented room furnished with a single bed in which four people slept – Michelangelo, the servant and his boy Pietro, Lapo and Lodovico. But a letter to his brother Buonarroto, dated December 19, 1506, painfully reveals the life of those days: «... to come here Giovan Simone I do not advise it yet, because I am here in a poor room and I have bought only one bed, in which we four persons lie, and I would be unable to welcome you properly...».

A month later, Giovan Simone still insisting on visiting him, Michelangelo wrote back annoyed to his elder brother, «...I don't want you to come here before I cast the figure that I am making. You don't need to know why... I think by mid-Lent to be ready to cast my figure so pray God that it comes well...».

But the assistants from Florence soon proved disappointing. Lapo turned out to be scoundrel, a thief and a braggart. He went around saying that the statue was his, even though it was attributed to Michelangelo; and having been charged with procuring the wax for the casting, he made Michelangelo pay a higher price, pocketing the difference. As soon as he realized this Michelangelo threw him out of the house.

«Eight ducats a month and expenses wasn't enough for him, that still he schemed to cheat me», wrote Michelangelo bitterly to his father. But Lapo had a strong influence over Lodovico Lotti. Returning to Florence he took his companion with him, leaving the sculptor alone and in difficulty.

The Pope was now spreading the word that the air of Bologna was bad for his health. In reality he was worried because the King of France had moved against Genoa, and had decided to return to Rome. After a last visit to Michelangelo, having left for him a thousand *scudi* in the bank of Messer Antonmaria da Lignano, he rushed away by the fastest road, not even stopping in Florence as everyone had expected.

Remaining alone, Michelangelo began to search for new assistants who were above all expert foundrymen. Once again he beseeched the Signoria of Florence, writing to his friend Angiolo Malfidi, Herald of the Republic, to send him master Bernardino son of master Antonio, foundryman of the Florence artillery. Master Bernardino arrived at Bologna in May. In late June the statue of Julius II was cast in bronze, with disastrous results.

«It is enough to say», wrote Michelangelo bitterly to his brother Buonarroto, «that the thing came badly. Let God be thanked, because I think everything for the best».

It had happened that master Bernardino, either through ignorance or by accident, had not smelted the bronze well, so that most of the metal had remained in the furnace. Consequently, the statue had been cast only up to the belt. «I would have believed that Master Bernardino», the letter went on, «was able to smelt without fire, so great was my faith in him;

nonetheless, it is not that he is not a good master or that he has not worked with love. But who makes it, let him make it».

A new casting was prepared to complete the figure, pouring the bronze over the part already cast. This time everything went well. The statue came out whole, although it had to be cleaned all over.

Poor Michelangelo. Working «with the greatest discomfort and with extreme fatigue» and suffering so much «that I would not believe I had enough life in me», and even convinced that only «the prayers of some person have helped me», must surely have remembered more than once his heedless, mean criticism of Leonardo, who had been unable to cast in a single piece a statue four times larger than that of Julius II.

Michelangelo was intent on cleaning the bronze statue before its official inauguration when Francesco Francia suddenly appeared before him. He had pulled strings to have himself received, his curiosity aroused by the praise for that work to be heard all over Bologna. Francia was a goldsmith and sculptor, as well as a painter, and was considered the best among all the artists of Bologna. Accompanied by a large group of gentlemen, he abruptly invaded Michelangelo's studio.

«What do you think of it?», Michelangelo asked him.

Francia, unable or unwilling to answer explicitly, replied that the casting seemed to have been successful and that he judged the material to be particularly beautiful.

«If this is beautiful material I must be grateful to Pope Julius, who gave it to me, like you to the shopkeepers who give you the colors», replied Michelangelo, offended.

Francia, stung to the quick in the presence of his fellow citizens and admirers, hotly replied. And Michelangelo answered by grabbing him roughly and pushing him out of the door: «Go to the bordello», he cried, «you and Cossa, both of you blunderers in art!».

A few days later some of those gentlemen, happening to meet Michelangelo again, asked him:

«What weighs more, Messer Michelagnolo, your statue of the Pope or a pair of oxen? We were just discussing this».

«It depends on the oxen», the artist replied seriously. «Those of Florence are certainly inferior to your Bologna ones».

In the group was a handsome boy, attractive and intelligent, and they presented him to the artist:

«This is Francia's son».

«I see that your father,» said Michelangelo with a caress, «makes more beautiful figures alive than painted. Tell him I said so».

Finally the monument was ready to be unveiled before the people.

A Bolognese chronicler speaks of this inauguration: «In 1508, February 21, at the time of 15 by astrological point, was unveiled the bronze statue of Pope Julius Second, seated, with the throne on his head, his right hand imparting benediction and the other holding the keys. It was placed at the greater door of San Petronio on the outside...».

Keys, then, not a sword. Michelangelo had beautifully resolved the dilemma of the Pope's left hand, leaving the severity of a warrior to be indicated only in the expression of the face.

That statue, although cast in bronze and destined to challenge the centuries, had a very short life.

In 1511 Bentivoglio re-entered Bologna victorious. The Pope's statue was torn down and the bronze was melted down to make a cannon, which was called, in contempt of the Pope, «the Julia».

On the day after the inauguration Michelangelo left for Florence. Someone, whose name is unknown, must certainly have wept; an obscure Bolognese girl whom we can imagine only for Michelangelo's poetic description of her in a sonnet jotted down on the back of letter. She had blond hair, a garland of flowers on her head, a dress «that binds the breast, then billows out», a belt that seemed glad to encircle that waist. And the artist in love concluded:

Now what then will my arms hold?

There is no other indication, no indiscretion. If Michelangelo really loved, as there is good reason to believe, that love remained a secret from all. Another love, much more absolute, dominated him and was to dominate him his whole life through: his art.

In late February 1508 the sculptor arrived home. His father and brothers were anxiously awaiting him, or rather awaiting his earnings and the help he had promised Buonarroto and Giovan Simone. Convinced that this would be a long stay, he rented for a year the house that the Opera del Duomo had had built for him years ago by Cronaca, at the time when he was to sculpt the twelve Apostles.

Soderini, content to have him back again, wrote to Alberigo Malaspina, the Marquis of Carrara, asking him to conserve a certain piece of marble that Michelangelo had blocked out on site to make a Hercules that would be placed in the square facing the David.

But the Pope, having been informed that the sculptor was in Florence, sent to call for him. Michelangelo promptly obeyed, not so much in the hope of continuing the tomb, an idea now abandoned by Julius II, as to show his submission and convince the Pope, who was thinking of commissioning paintings from him, that painting was not his art. What awaited him, instead, was the vault of the Sistine Chapel.

It will look poor

AN EVIL THOUGHT may give rise to some good work, and a wrong action to a masterpiece. When this happens it is usually attributed to chance, lucky or unlucky, providential or deplorable, although chance does not really exist. Man always obeys his deepest impulses, and character is fate.

Bramante, jealous of Michelangelo and the favor the Pope had shown him again in Bologna, had an idea that was as simple as it was clever.

Item one: if the Pope should decide to continue building his tomb, a good part of the money allocated for the new Basilica of Saint Peter's would go for the marble, ending up in Michelangelo's pocket and not Bramante's.

Item two: if Michelangelo begins working on the tomb again, the Pope will go to see him every day and will consult his friend about every decision.

Item three: Michelangelo is a surly man who won't listen to reason. With him it is impossible to come to terms. He is an intransigent, incorruptible complainer, a «fox without a tail» who sees and knows too much, even things he shouldn't know, about certain misdeeds committed by Bramante.

Consequently, it will be necessary to make trouble for him. How? By having him produce work that is mediocre, not sculpture, to embarrass him before the Pope. To belittle the «divine» Michelangelo, considered the greatest sculptor not only of his day but of all time, the only solution was to lure him into an art that was not his: that of painting.

Bramante, with the skill of a courtier, worked on the Pope day by day, instilling in him a great desire to see his Michelangelo at work in the Sistine Chapel, grappling with paintbrushes and colors.

After Michelangelo's inevitable failure the Pope, in the

scheming plans of Bramante, would have consoled himself at once with the young Raphael, who was already frescoing the Dispute of the Sacrament, to the wonder and admiration of all Rome.

But Bramante had not accounted for one thing: genius. At the Pope's insistence, and knowing how his enemies would gloat over a no that would anger the Pope, or a yes that would endanger his fame, Michelangelo accepted the challenge.

In the first project the vault of the chapel was to have twelve apostles, represented in the lunettes, and some decoration. «Then, having begun this work, I thought it would be a poor thing, and I told the Pope that, making the apostles alone, it would seem poor. He asked me, why? I said because they were poor themselves. So he gave me a new commission, that I was to do what I wanted...».

In little more than two years, working alone, Michelangelo frescoed the vault of the chapel (over three hundred square meters) narrating in a wonderful, luminous synthesis the entire Old Testament, from the creation of the world and of life to the creation of man and woman, from the first sin to the expulsion from Paradise, from the flood to the new humankind of Noah. Through the prophets and sibyls, he then depicted all of Christ's ancestors up to the eve of his coming.

Genius exploded at last, in joy and grief, surpassing any possible foreshadowing, transcending its very self.

The retort to Bramante was a masterpiece that has never been equaled. The greatest sculptor of the age suddenly revealed himself as the greatest painter of his century.

This then was to be the conclusion. It was preceded by all the stages of that ordeal that began when the Pope first persuaded Michelangelo to climb up on the scaffolding and later, with the usual impetus of his fiery nature, told him to climb down again before he threw him off it.

«Holiness, I tell you this is not my art, and that I am not experienced in colors».

«And I tell you that you will do it anyway and it will be a worthy thing».

«But I am a sculptor, Holy Father. Assign this chapel to Raphael. He is a young man of great talent, they say he has already done excellent things in Florence and Perugia».

«Michelangelo, you will paint the vault of the chapel, unless you want to provoke my anger again».

«I will paint the chapel, Holy Father».

Bramante was ordered to construct the scaffolding, which he erected by hanging it from the ceiling on great ropes.

«And when I have finished painting», Michelangelo asked him, «how will we plug those holes?»

«Don't worry. We'll think about it then. We can't do it any other way».

«We can instead. If you don't know how, I'll teach you myself».

Michelangelo went to the Pope and, in the presence of Bramante, described all the defects of that scaffolding, obtaining permission to make it over in his own way. Instead of hanging it from the ceiling he had it rest on *sorgozzoni*, or beams projecting from the windows like props. From then on Bramante was to adopt the same system.

Now it was time to finish the cartoons and start painting. With the money the Pope had given him he could afford to use assistants, as his master Domenico del Ghirlandaio had done; and Michelangelo turned to his friends from the workshop, writing to the faithful Granacci.

A friend in need is a friend indeed, as an old proverb says, and Granacci wasted no time. He rounded up a squadron of artists, all expert in fresco work, to whom Michelangelo offered twenty ducats a head as a first payment on account, to be calculated as part of the salary for those who remained after the trial.

The painters, in addition to Granacci himself, were: Giuliano Bugiardini, Jacopo di Sandro, Indaco the Elder, Agnolo di Donnino and Bastiano da Sangallo known as Aristotile.

They were all Florentine artists, more or less successful and well-known, who willingly and immediately interrupted their work, defying the anger of their clients, to hurry to Michelangelo in his hour of need. Granacci and Bugiardini were companions from the time of Ghirlandaio and the Magnificent. Jacopo di Sandro del Tedesco was not as close to Michelangelo, but they were well acquainted. The same was true of Indaco and Agnolo di Donnino, disciple and friend of Cosimo Rosselli. They were all old acquaintances except for one, the youngest and most «michelangelesque» of all, Bastiano da Sangallo, grandson of the architect Giuliano. He had been working with Perugino at the Santissima Annunziata when he saw the cartoons for the Battle of Cascina. They were truly «the school of the world» in the words of Cellini, and for the young Bastiano they represented the road to Damascus. Dazzled by Michelangelo's genius, he left Perugino and fervently set to work copying the cartoons. In doing so he described their anatomical secrets with such competence and skill, commenting on them with such perception, that he was given the nickname of «Aristotile».

The band of Florentines arrived at Rome. Michelangelo, with the cartoons of the apostles already finished, had them begin some figures as a trial. The results were disappointing. It was not what the artist had expected.

One morning, arriving at the chapel at daybreak, long before his friends, Michelangelo felt a moment of despair. After taking a long look, increasingly dissatisfied, at the few square meters of fresco that were drying, he abruptly overturned the paints, scraped away everything his assistants had done, climbed down from the scaffolding, strode to the door and turned the key in the lock.

The assistants arrived a little later. Finding the door locked they began to knock and call. Michelangelo refused to open and refused to answer. Thinking it was a joke played by their friend and master, still known as a ferocious *uccellatore*, they returned later, but in vain. They waited for evening and went to the artist's home, but he refused to reply to them. Next morning they returned to the chapel. Finally they understood that Michelangelo was serious, and wished to see them no more.

Offended and embittered, they returned to Florence.

It was not an admirable gesture. Now, with the frescos of the vault before our eyes, we can only admit that it was necessary. But those painters who had come running at his call could have been dismissed in a different way, without the insult of the door locked in their faces and the refusal to give any explanation. Perhaps Michelangelo preferred to offend them rather than humiliate them; to have himself condemned as friend so as not to condemn them as artists.

Alone now, fiercely alone, without even an assistant to grind the colors, he confronted the immense naked ceiling of the Sistine Chapel, beginning everything anew.

We enter the Chapel now and lift our eyes, as millions of amazed spectators have done before us and will do after us, in a silence more eloquent than applause.

We see the architectural framing of that volt and begin to decipher it until, overcome by emotion, we are forced to stop. In the nine panels of the ceiling we see God who divides light from darkness, who creates the sun and the moon, the animals and plants, who stretches out his hand to man, calling him to life. Then comes the birth of woman, the temptation of the serpent with a human face, Eve so like our own women, beautiful and determined in the awareness of guilt, the expulsion from paradise where Masaccio's lesson is re-experienced and renovated, the sacrifice of Noah, the flood with the first tangled mass of bodies anticipating the Last Judgement, and finally the drunkenness of Noah, the profaning of his sleep.

Between one panel and the other, on marble bases, twenty nude figures, twenty graceful young men beautiful as demigods stand as solitary, timeless witnesses of the tragic and eternal beauty of Adam.

Between one niche and another are the prophets and sibyls, God's spokesmen. Lastly, as if cowering in the lunettes, are the ancestors of Christ.

The Chapel evokes stupefaction and consternation. A lifetime, and that of one man alone, would not have been enough to complete that vast undertaking.

Michelangelo spread the plaster, meter by meter, painting the background before it dried, in total solitude. Unable to verify the effect of the foreshortened figures by looking at them from below, he had to imagine it from his place on the scaffolding, from which he could not descend. For a year he took his meals and slept up there. If he received letters he had to lean backward to read them, being unable to hold his head straight. And there were petulant messages from his father and brothers that called him back to earth, to the meanness of everyday human life. He answered with explosions of rage and affection, but from above, from «up there», where even his body had now taken on a grotesque shape, always bent like a bow, with head rolled backward, belly protruding, and twisted back.

«... I am supposed to love myself more than others, and I cannot make use of the things necessary to me...».

«... I am here in great labor, and with very great bodily fatigue, and I have no friends of any sort nor do I want them; and I do not have enough time to eat what I need. But let me not be given any more annoyance, for I could not bear another ounce of it...».

Alone by choice. The Pope had had a stepladder constructed so that he could visit him. Occasionally he surprised Michelangelo, his face disfigured by the paint dripping onto it and into his eyes, closed tight in a silence that might seem that of madness. This was the «price of glory», the weight that heavily bore down the other side of the scales.

He was helped, at home more than in the chapel, by the faithful Pietro Basso, who had been with him in Bologna too. But Pietro suddenly came down with fever and had to return home at death's door.

Back in Florence, the reckless Giovan Simone had threatened and offended old Lodovico. It was reported to Michelangelo. By now he was the head of the household to whom everyone, his father first of all, turned with childish petulance.

«Giovansimone. They say that if you treat a good man well it makes him even better, and if you treat a wicked one so it makes him worse. ... I don't say that you are wicked but you are acting in a way that I don't like... I am not even certain whether you are really my brother, because if you were, you would not threaten my father. I will treat you like an animal... I have been, for twelve years now, living a life of misery all over Italy; supporting every shame; suffering every hardship; endangering my life a thousand times, only to help my family; and now that I have begun to raise our house up again a little, you alone will be the one to destroy it and ruin in one hour what I have achieved in so many years and with such fatigue. By the body of Christ, that is the truth! And I am ready to confound ten thousand like you...».

It was a crescendo of rage and passion: like the drama of the chapel.

«Holy Father, I told you this was not my art. Everything I have done is spoiled. If you don't believe me, send someone to see».

Michelangelo had begun the panel of the Flood when he realized that the painting was becoming covered with mould, so thick that the figures were no longer visible.

At once the Pope sent Giuliano da Sangallo to inspect the work. Sangallo observed that the mortar was too liquid. Evaporating, it caused that phenomenon, which was not however harmful to the fresco.

More and more often, Julius II climbed the scaffolding to observe the work of Michelangelo. The artist had already frescoed half of the vault, starting from the side furthest from the altar and nearest to the door.

«Michelangelo, when will it be finished?»

«Holiness, when I am able to finish it».

«But in the meantime let's uncover it, so it can be seen».

And the Pope had the scaffolding taken down.

It was August 14, 1511. If Michelangelo had begun to paint, as is probable, in January of 1509, only twenty months had passed.

Artists as well as dignitaries from the Curia swarmed to see the work. Curiosity was immense, also because the surly artist had forbidden anyone to enter the chapel before.

The judgement was unanimous: the painter Michelangelo was fully equal to the sculptor Michelangelo. And envy was equally great. Bramante tried to persuade the Pope to commission Raphael to paint the other half of the vault.

On hearing of this Michelangelo rushed to the Pope and told him in Bramante's presence that he would not stand for such an insult. He then informed Julius II of the «crimes» committed by that intriguing architect, who in the excitement of constructing a new basilica had vandalized the old one. He had thrown down and broken columns instead of removing them carefully. He had stolen from the Pope's pockets by turning to his own profit the sums destined to the Fabric of Saint Peter's and scrimping on materials, as was now apparent in the basilica itself, in the corridor of the Belvedere, in San Pietro in Vincoli and other buildings where the walls were crumbling and all of the foundations had had to be reinforced.

Julius II, highly perturbed, comforted Michelangelo and urged him to finish frescoing the vault. The scaffolding was erected again and Michelangelo returned to his isolation from the world, no longer distinguishing day from night or feast days from working days.

Months passed.

«Holiness, I want to go to Florence for Saint John's Day. Will you give me leave?»

«And when will you finish this chapel?»

«Your Holiness, when I'm able».

«When I'm able! When I'm able!» yelled the Pope, striking Michelangelo on the shoulder with the stick he always carried. «You want me to throw you down from that scaffolding!».

Michelangelo, having decided to flee a second time, and this time for good, climbed down from the scaffolding and went home.

«You wan't throw me down», he muttered to himself as he prepared to leave for Florence, «because I'm not going back up there again».

At that moment a knock was heard at the door. It was a gentleman from the court of Julius II bringing him a bag with five hundred ducats in it, and the Pope's apologies.

Michelangelo went to Florence, but came back soon and set to work again.

«Michelangelo, when are you going to finish this blessed chapel?».

The Pope incessantly climbed the ladder to examine from nearby, one by one, all of the figures, to the great annoyance of the artist.

«Soon, Holy Father, probably before Christmas».

But before the Pope could come back again the artist had had all of the scaffolding taken down.

On All Saints Day of 1512 the vault was uncovered. The Pope was informed and hurried at once to see it. It still had to be touched up with ultramarine and with gold.

«Why don't you touch it up?»

«Because it's good like this».

«And yet», continued the Pope, «I think it needs touching up with gold».

«I don't see, Holy Father, that men are covered with gold».

«It will look poor».

«Those who are painted here, Holy Father, were poor themselves».

The Pope understood, and could only agree.

Lonely as a hangman

WHILE MICHELANGELO WAS painting the vault of the Sistine chapel, Raphael was frescoing the Stanze in the Vatican. Bramante, in his jealousy, had unwittingly provoked this highest challenge, on the same level as the one conceived years before by the Gonfalonier of Florence when he called Leonardo and Michelangelo to execute the cartoons for the battles.

Michelangelo had been younger then. In comparison with Leonardo's almost legendary fame, he was the still primitive, instinctive genius who in a sudden impetus had created the colossus in the square. Now instead the younger man was Raphael, handsome and well-mannered, for whom painting was a joyous mode of expression; as much as it was, on the contrary, a tragedy for Michelangelo.

Julius II, setting them to compete, knew that neither of the two would have surpassed the other, being so different in temperament and artistic language. But each of the two, in this auspicious competition, would have surpassed himself.

In Florence Raphael had carefully studied the cartoons for the Battle of Cascina. In Rome, with the complicity of Bramante, he had more than once managed to get a glimpse of Michelangelo's work. Moreover, he was able to examine it as his ease when Julius II had the scaffolding taken down. But no one could accuse Raphael of imitating Michelangelo. Undoubtedly, he was impressed. Michelangelo's work was new and grandiose, his drawings showing a knowledge of anatomy never seen before; and Raphael drew from it the lesson he needed. He neither copied nor imitated, but looked and assimilated, employing what he learned to perfection.

From the *Disputation on the Sacrament* to the *School of Athens* a plastic expansion of space can be observed in the figures, more fluently drawn, and in a freer use of foreshortening. In similar manner, in Michelangelo's Sistine Chapel there can be observed, between the drunkenness of Noah (the panel nearest to the door) and the creation of light (the one nearest the altar), an artistic maturation not limited to a greater mastery of pictorial means but implying a constant endeavor to achieve a synthesis that concludes in absolute perfection in the panel dedicated to the creation of Adam.

A biographer recounts that «Raphael being one day in company of his disciples, he met Michelangelo who asked him: "Where are you going, Raphael, accompanied like a Monsignor?". And Raphael retorted: "And you, alone as a hangman?"».

Not as a hangman, but as a sad and lonely one, was Raphael to depict the meditative Michelangelo, in the garb of the philosopher Heraclites. It was homage paid to his master and rival, an open acknowledgment of his admiration.

Balls! Balls!

WHILE THE TWO greatest painters of the Renaissance were conducting their highly civilized battle in Rome, things were going badly for the Republic in Florence, and the news added another sorrow to Michelangelo's burden of care.

Julius II had never forgotten the offense of the Florentines who, in addition to having remained faithful to the King of France, had allowed Pisa to play host to a *conciliabolo* of schismatic cardinals. The Pope thundered an interdiction against the Florentine Republic, which the discontented factions immediately tried to exploit to their advantage. As enemies of the Gonfalonier they proclaimed themselves, rightly or wrongly, friends of the Medici. Having weathered the defeat of Ravenna, Julius II had managed to put together a league against France, and had asked Lorenzo Pucci in Florence to provide concrete help in the form of financing.

Florence tried to get out of it by delaying. But time was working against the hesitant city. The league against France, meeting at Mantova, decided to wage war on Florence, and Don Raimondo Cardona, the Viceroy of Naples, marched on Tuscany at the head of Spanish troops.

This army was to perpetrate the famous, or rather infamous, sack of Prato. Under the eyes of the papal delegate over five thousand persons were killed in a single night, and the acts of sacrilege and rape were countless. «They sacked all Prato», wrote a terrified chronicler, «that is, all of the houses and all of the churches and convents of the monks and nuns, and they had no regard for any person, either in killing them or in committing other things...».

This news aroused the souls of the Florentines who, it was said, had «their guts in a bucket».

Pier Soderini fled by night from the palace and the city, first pretending to go to Rome and then, perhaps having received a message from his brother the Cardinal, taking ship to seek refuge in Ragusa. The Florentines, frightened and confused, tried to negotiate with the besiegers by reconstituting the government. Cardinal Giovanni de' Medici and his brother Giuliano returned to the palace in Via Larga as private citizens; only briefly, however, enough time to gather together the conspirators who had remained faithful to them. Then the cry was heard once more: «*Palle! Palle!*».

Palazzo della Signoria was occupied. All of the republican laws were overthrown and a war magistracy composed of the boldest *Palleschi*, the Medici partisans, was created.

From Rome Michelangelo wrote his family to comfort them, exhorting them to stay out of quarrels, authorizing them to draw money from his funds deposited at the hospice of Santa Maria Nuova, since in cases like this what counts is not gold but life «and do not become involved in any of the cases of the earth, either in facts or in words, but do as is done in plague time, be the first to flee».

Then when calm had been restored he wrote again to his brother Buonarroto: «... it is said that the house of Medici has returned to Florence and that everything is settled: for which I believe that the danger has ceased, that is as regards the Spaniards, and I do not think that you need to leave. But stay in peace and do not make a friend or intimate of anyone, except God...».

But the Buonarroti family, in Florence, were not left in peace by the *Palleschi*, who accused Michelangelo of having spoken against the Medici family. And here Michelangelo wrote again indignantly from Rome, a letter to comfort his father: «You must have patience... for never have I found people more ungrateful nor more haughty than the Florentines», and one addressed directly to Giuliano.

By the end of that tumultuous year of 1512, the Buonarroti family had been re-established or, as was then said «reblessed» and the vault of the Sistine Chapel was solemnly inaugurated with a mass celebrated by the Pope on All Saints Day.

On February 21, 1513, like a soldier on the field of battle, Julius II died, declaring to the cardinals gathered at his bedside that he had never been able to govern the Church, nor to free Italy from the «barbarians», and calling himself the greatest of all sinners.

Weeping he left the tomb

B UT THE TERRIBLE old man had not forgotten his terrible friend. In his will Julius had ordered that Michelangelo finish his tomb without delay.

His executors – his nephew Cardinal Leonardo Grossi della Rovere, bishop of Agen and the Protonotary Apostolic Lorenzo Pucci – stipulated with the artist a new contract pledging him to finish the tomb within seven years. There would still be forty statues, but only three faces to the monument instead of four, since it was to rest against the wall. The stipulated recompense was sixteen thousand and five hundred gold ducats, of which two hundred were to be paid at the signing of the agreement.

At last Michelangelo was not obliged to produce immediately, and could dedicate himself wholly to his art. He called for assistants from Florence, now possessing the means to pay them. Almost certainly he made several trips to Carrara to select more blocks of marble to be used in the monument.

Shortly after the death of Julius II, the «little Cardinal» Giovanni de' Medici had been elected Pope, taking the name of Leo X. The news, report witnesses, arrived at Florence «by air», transmitted by the jubilant bonfires lit to signal it from one castle to the next. Florence itself seemed ready to burst into flames of joy.

The new Pope was thirty-seven years old. Plump, smiling, easy-going but not simple, he was by nature peace-loving and good-hearted but above all, for Michelangelo and for the people of Florence, he was the son of the Magnificent, almost one of the family.

The Pope immediately appointed archbishop of Florence his cousin Giulio, the illegitimate son of the handsome Giu-

103

liano, victim of the Pazzi conspiracy. He called Soderini back from exile and exhorted the Signoria to free all political prisoners, among them Machiavelli.

«Among so many hundreds of our fellow citizens who in these times have come to render homage», said the new Pope one day to his courtiers, «we have found only one truly wise and only one truly mad. The first is Pier Soderini who, leaving aside any private interest, has instantaneously recommended to us the city of Fiorenza; the other is the jester Carafulla, who has made us the same recommendation».

Raphael became the favorite artist of Leo X. Michelangelo remained what he had been in the old days in Via Larga, a bad-tempered brother. In the early months of his pontificate Leo let Michelangelo work on the tomb of his predecessor. In 1513 Michelangelo probably sculpted the *Captives* now in the Louvre, and may have already begun the *Moses* as well, when he received a visit from the aged Luca Signorelli.

«I am not well, dear Luca, and I cannot even work», said Michelangelo showing the painter «a figure in marble, erect, four *braccia* high, that had its hands behind it», that is, the dying captive.

«Have no doubt, Michelagnolo, the angels will come down from heaven to take your arms and help you».

The aged Signorelli, who had already painted that *Last Judgement* in the Duomo of Orvieto that Michelangelo loved, had come to Rome from Cortona for an audience with the Pope. Then, finding himself without money, he had gone to ask a loan from his solitary fellow townsman.

«I being at Rome in the first year of Pope Leo, there came Maestro Luca da Cortona painter, ...he told me that he had come to speak to the Pope to get I remember not what, and that he had risked having his head cut off for love of the Medici family, and that it seemed to him that this was not acknowledged... He asked me for forty *iuli*... and having taken that money he went with God...».

On trips to Carrara Michelangelo was glad to stop in Florence, inquiring about his brother Buonarroto's business and passionately participating in the events of the city.

In search of a boy to help him with the housework, he asked Buonarroto to find him someone «willing to serve» in exchange for room and board, a salary and some lessons. But then finding himself burdened with a petulant, demanding boy, he wrote dismally to his father: «... Oh, this is all I needed! Now I have this little turd of a boy who says he doesn't want to waste time, but wants to learn... and wants to stay up all night drawing».

In April of 1515, during one of these visits to Florence, he was shown a bit of balcony that Baccio d'Agnolo had added, as a trial, around Brunelleschi's dome.

«It's a crude thing», exclaimed the sculptor. «It looks like a cage for crickets!».

This biting criticism spread all over town: «Michelangelo says it's a cage for crickets!».

«You show us what should be done, then», retorted the designers of the balcony.

«I will show you».

The artist set to work, and presented his own model. Cardinal Giulio appointed a committee of experts to judge it. Michelangelo's project was rejected, but Baccio d'Agnolo was also prevented from completing his balcony. Today it can be seen just as it was left, a fragment visible on the Via del Proconsolo side of the Duomo.

Toward the end of that year the Pope, traveling to Bologna to meet the new King of France Francis I, stopped in Florence, where he was welcomed with the highest honors. After having prayed before the tomb of his father in San Lorenzo he conceived the idea of having the greatest artists compete in a project for the facade of the church. Baccio d'Agnolo, Giuliano da Sangallo, Andrea and Jacopo Sansovino and Raphael, who always accompanied the Pope, were invited to participate. Michelangelo, whether invited or not we do not know, entered the competition; and won.

A year later the Pope sent to call for him. It was Winter, and for months the sculptor had been staying in Carrara, where he had rented a house in order to supervise the quarrying of marble for the tomb of Julius II.

«My dear Michelangelo», said Leo X, «I would like to see another drawing of the facade, one that will have ten statues: four below, four above and the last two at the top. Those at the bottom should represent, starting from the Canto alla Paglia and going toward the Canto alla Macina, Saint Lawrence, Saint John the Baptist, Saint Peter and Saint Paul, that is those who testified to the truth through martyrdom. Those above should represent Saint Luke, Saint John the Evangelist, Saint Matthew and Saint Mark, who testified to the truth through words. Those at the top should represent our own saints Saint Cosimo and Saint Damiano, and it should be obvious that they were physicians. Make me this drawing at once and bring it to me».

Two weeks later the artist presented the Pope with a new project. Cardinal Giulio was also present and both of them openly expressed great satisfaction.

«Now you will go to Carrara for the marble, and as soon as you can you will give me a model in wood».

«Holy Father», replied Michelangelo, «I have just renewed another contract with Cardinals Pucci and Della Rovere for the tomb of Pope Julius, in which they forbid me to accept any other commitment until I have finished it».

«Don't worry about that, I will send for them and I will content them. You will not have to work on the facade, we will have it supervised by Baccio d'Agnolo. You must think only of the statues, that must all be from your hand alone. And then, when you are in Florence, you will still have the time and means to make some statues for that tomb as well».

Michelangelo had learned by now, through painful experience, that a pope is not to be contradicted. Bitterly he bowed his head once more. He had loved the violent old Julius II, and the Pope had felt the same affection for him.

Now he would have to pay his debt, make him a tomb worthy of the grandeur of he who had wished it and he who had conceived it. But just when the marble was available again and he could have dedicated himself to creating those statues, he had to go back to Carrara.

Michelangelo wept. He confessed it, in his old age, to his disciple and biographer, who wrote: «Weeping he left the tomb and went back to Florence».

The bickering of monks

WHEN LEO X acceded to Saint Peter's throne in 1513, the Pope's treasury was depleted. Years of war, armies to be maintained, alliances to be bought, plus the natural prodigality of his predecessor with his grandiose projects for his tomb and for the new Basilica, had exhausted the reserves. The Medici Pope was faced with the urgent need to obtain new funds; and he thought the best way to do so was to have them rain down from heaven. By what miracle? By that of selling indulgences.

Two papal bulls dated October 1517 granted total remission from sin to those who carried out the works prescribed for the Jubilee, or who – if they could not come to Rome – donated money to rebuild the Basilica.

Indulgence was also granted to souls in Purgatory, so that the faithful could, with an appropriate offering, extend it to deceased members of the family.

The preaching of indulgence was organized with great care in the territory of Germany, from which the Roman church expected the highest returns, and the Archbishop of Magonza entrusted it to the oratory of the Dominican fathers. Even a famous bank in Augsburg, the Fugger, which had branches in almost every German city, collaborated in the campaign to collect and transfer the money, opening special branches where indulgence certificates, signed and stamped, were consigned upon payment in cash.

There were fixed rates for persons and for sins. The highest social classes such as princes, archbishops and bishops paid, for absolution, 25 gold florins; prelates, counts, barons, 10 florins; wealthy merchants, 9 florins; those of average income, 6 florins; shopkeepers, 1 florin; and the poor, half a florin. There were fixed rates for sins too: 12 ducats for sodomy, 7 for sacrilege, 6 for witchcraft, 4 for parricide, and so on down the scale to half a ducat.

The undertaking, launched as a real crusade mobilizing the entire clergy, met with the resentment of the people and the disgust of the Augustinians.

This religious sentiment, «offended and scandalized», found its spokesman in a young Augustinian monk, teacher of philosophy and theology at the University of Wittenberg, who wrote 95 theses against the sale of indulgences and affixed them to the door of the castle church. The date was the eve of All Saints Day of 1517, and the monk was Martin Luther.

An earthquake would not have had a more devastating effect. All Germany was shaken to the roots. Luther's theses spread like wildfire. The indulgence market collapsed. A Dominican, taking up the challenge, replied with 110 anti-theses, but in vain. The people were on Luther's side. Still proclaiming himself a catholic, Luther sent the Pope his «Resolutions» in which he stated «... he who denies alms to the poor and buys indulgences incurs the wrath of God», and concluded, «...Prostrated at the feet of Your Holiness, I offer myself to you with everything I have and am. Scourge me, kill me, call me, revoke me, approve me, disapprove me, as you will. I will recognize in your voice the voice of Christ who presides in you and speaks».

When Leo X was informed of these impassioned discussions, he idly commented, «The bickering of monks», another of those theological disputes that were so frequent and so vehement in Medieval times. The Pope failed to understand, or was not informed, that the discussion – unlike the medieval ones, restricted to monasteries or universities – had come out of the church into the public square. Luther's theses, touching on the quick a financial issue of general interest, aroused a direct, passionate reaction from the people, with immediate political and social implications.

The Elector of Saxony approved Luther's propositions, and the nobility followed in his steps. The medium-and small-scale merchants refused to pay the tribute. The Augustinians organized a conference in Heidelberg with a public debate. Luther, encouraged by the approval of the people, challenged the attacks of five doctors in theology and emerged triumphant from this severe trial. The question of indulgences had now become an insurrection, the *protest* of all of Germany against the catholic Church. Leo X, alarmed, issued a bull of excommunication against Luther. The monk replied by burning the bull in the public square.

Michelangelo, of course, ignored these dramatic events, unlike Raphael to whom the Pope confided all his worries. Isolated in the Apuane mountains amid simple, unsophisticated people, he felt their reflection only in the Pope's fast-changing moods. Once he was even accused of seeking his own interest in buying marble, because he bought at Carrara (an independent territory) rather than at Pietrasanta (under the dominion of Florence). A severe, admonishing letter from Giulio de' Medici ordered him, in the name of the Pope, to change quarry. And he obeyed. But there was no road to transport the marble from the mountains to the sea, so he had to act as engineer, building a difficult, expensive road, carved out of rock, since political reasons demanded it. In doing so he made an enemy of the Marquis of Carrara and provoked the hatred of the Carrara marble quarriers, who threatened and sabotaged him.

«...A link in the chain that held the column broke, and the column crashed into the river in a hundred pieces. We all, everyone around it, were in very great danger of our lives...».

At times he wrote to his powerful friend Domenico Buoninsegni, knowing that his words would reach the ear of Pope Leo, and reconfirmed his awareness of his own value: «...I have the will to construct the facade of San Lorenzo, that it will be, in architecture and in sculpture, the mirror of all Italy...».

Once already, when Michelangelo had just arrived in Rome, Cardinal Riario, showing him his collection of statues, had asked if he had it in him to do something of the kind. That time he had left his reply to the proofs he would have given. Now, without conceit but with honest certainty, he promised from the Apuanes a facade in which Renaissance Italy could mirror itself for centuries to come.

A sinister prediction

T HE FACADE, HOWEVER, was not built, and the church of San Lorenzo is still waiting for it, or rather waiting no longer, since it has been sculpted by centuries of weathering that have faded the red brick and white plaster to warm tones of gray and moss-green.

Michelangelo wasted precious years in Carrara, while in Rome his place was being taken by Raphael. In 1514 Bramante had died, warmly recommending his pupil to the Pope. Raphael had thus become the Supervisor of Works of the Fabric of Saint Peter's. Sebastiano del Piombo, jealous of the painter from Urbino, sent Michelangelo news of the court, enlivened with acrid comments on his fortunate young rival.

«I am sorry... you are not in Rome to see two paintings of those sent to France by the Prince of the Synagogue [an allusion to Raphael]..., since I believe you could not imagine anything more contrary to your own opinion...».

When not in Carrara Michelangelo was in Florence working on the statues for the tomb of Julius II. He had also accepted a commission to sculpt a nude Christ, life size, for Metello Vari, but in working on it had found a dark vein in the marble that spoiled it. Unwillingly he made another one, leaving the first to be finished, and ruined, by his assistant Pietro Urbano. By now Rome was for him a myth, remote and unattainable.

He wrote to friends and enemies. The replies he received were sometimes comforting, sometimes offensive, like the one from Sansovino: «...cursed be the day that you ever spoke well of anyone». And in solitude and suffering, feeling more deeply than ever, he turned to poetry.

But Cardinal Giulio de' Medici was not the man to let his friend Michelangelo grow sad in idleness. After the Pope had

abandoned the idea of the facade, Giulio asked Michelangelo to make him a drawing for a chapel in San Lorenzo that
would hold the family tombs: those of his father Giuliano and
his uncle Lorenzo the Magnificent, as well as those of Giuliano Duke of Nemours and Lorenzo Duke of Urbino, who
had died recently.

Michelangelo made a drawing that pleased the Cardinal,
«and therefore, *amice noster carissime*, you will go on with
this work, as we strongly urge you to do».

From Rome arrived the news of the death of Raphael. At
the age of thirty-seven he died on his birthday, Good Friday
of 1520. The Pope, it was said, wept in greater despair than
if for a brother or a son.

A year later came another death, that of Leo X.

Lastly, again from Rome, came the third bad tidings for
the Florentines. Cardinal Giulio had not been elected Pope,
and Peter's throne was now occupied by a Flemish priest,
Hadrian Bayers, who took the name of Hadrian VI.

But less than two years were to pass before the bells rang
out again in jubilation. In 1523, at the death of the Dutch
Pope the illegitimate son of Giuliano de' Medici, Cardinal
Giulio, was elected, taking the name of Clement VII.

In Florence the populace rejoiced. Even Michelangelo,
surprised by the news, felt he had to express his joy; and in
writing to a Carrara stonemason «...you will have heard», he
said, «how Medici has been made Pope: at which I think the
whole world is glad; and I believe that here, as regards art,
many things will be done». Only the most faithful and isolated of the Weepers, who had slunk back into shadow after
the death of Savonarola, anxiously recalled a sinister prediction of the friar who, asked by his jailer to state «when» the
dire calamities he had threatened would fall on Florence, had
replied: «In the time of Pope Clement».

Dante in the chapels

NOW MICHELANGELO HAD two tombs to complete: that of Julius II, with the Pope's heirs demanding that he finish and reproaching him for the money already paid, and that of the Medici, with the new chapel already built on the model of Brunelleschi's Old Sacristy and the statues already roughed out.

Michelangelo was exasperated by the nagging of the former and the interference of the latter. He even refused the monthly sum that the Pope had granted him, since fanatics in Rome had told him that, His Holiness having thought to assign him a lifetime pension, he should in their opinion become a lay brother, vowing never to marry.

Michelangelo wrote desperate letters to the Pope's friends and to the Pope himself. He even reached the point of saying «I struggle with poverty», while his surly, suspicious solitude was exasperated still further by the envy of artists such as Baccio Bandinelli and Sansovino, the jealousy of the Pope's courtiers and the ingratitude of his assistants.

«Piero», he wrote to Piero Gondi, «the poor ingrate has this nature; that if you satisfy his needs he says that what you give him was only what you didn't need yourself. If you put him to work to do him good, he says again that you were forced to do so, and since you didn't know how to do it yourself, you put him to it; and all the benefit he receives, he says that it is done to the advantage of the benefactor. And when the benefits received are so evident that they cannot be denied, the ingrate hopes that the one who has done him good will fall into some public error, that will cause him to be criticized, so as to release him from his own obligation...».

More that a heart-felt accusation, this is a bitterly profound analysis of the human soul. Were they not the words of Michelangelo, they could only have been those of Machiavelli. Forget about all those melancholy fantasies «provoked by those who do not wish you well», who try in this way to «turn you aside from this work, and, envious of your glory and well-being, to make you abandon the undertaking...», was the message sent him by Pope Clement VII.

The Medici Chapels mark the glorious conclusion of this obscure, tormented period. Now that we at last possess the key, we can decipher their great Christian message.

As in Brunelleschi's Old Sacristy, a pattern of squares and circles predominates in Michelangelo's New Sacristy. On the cube formed by the four walls, which represent the earth, rests the vault which represents the heavens. Between the cube and the vault however, Michelangelo inserted an intermediate plane that gives soaring height to this heaven.

To emphasize this upward soaring motion he designed the windows in the intermediate plane in the shape of a trapezoid, accentuating the perspective.

The nocturnal atmosphere is created by a severe and skillful distribution of the light that plays on the white walls and darkens in the shadow of the cornices.

We are in a tomb, not a church, where the atmosphere is funereal and the silence is more solemn.

On the wall where we enter is a seated Madonna holding her child. Beside her, resting on the same plane, are Saints Cosimo and Damiano, protectors of the Medici family. Facing the Madonna is the altar, designed according to the Ambrosian rite, with the priest facing the inside of the chapel. On the left wall is the tomb of Lorenzo Duke of Urbino, the son of Piero the Fatuous. He is depicted seated, wearing a helmet, his chin resting on hand in a meditative pose. Beneath him are the statues of Twilight and Dawn, turning away from him. On the right wall is the tomb of the youngest son of the Magnificent, Giuliano, Duke of Nemours and uncle of Lorenzo. He too is seated, his head bare, wearing an inlaid cuirass and holding a scepter lying across his knees. Below him are the statues of Day and Night. They too turn away from him.

Since the time of Michelangelo the statue of Night has been the dominant motif of the entire chapel. Night as the «shadow of death», the image of quiet and of rest, symbol and emblem of that other sleep without waking that is death.

At this point, to avoid falling into the romantic pitfall of this beautiful statue, we must open a parenthesis and go back to the time when Michelangelo, in the palace on Via Larga, first discovered Italian poetry.

Dante was unquestionably the poet most congenial to him, although like all of his contemporaries he considered Petrarch to be his master. Dante, in particular, he read almost every evening, for over a year, to the Bolognese gentlemen who had welcomed him to his home after the expulsion of Piero de' Medici from Florence. All his life, Dante and Savonarola, along with the Old and the New Testament, were to provide daily comfort for his solitude and nourishment for his thought.

Building a tomb for the two young dukes implied, for Michelangelo, a problem that was not merely aesthetic, but also moral. Who were these two men? He had known them well, and as a strict follower of Savonarola he could not say they had died in the odor of sanctity. They were two sinners surprised by death at an early age, leaving them no time for repentance. But the artist was also devoted to love, like Dante, and he knew that

> *...infinite Goodness has such great arms*
> *That she welcomes all those who turn to her.*

115

And who but the Madonna could turn to God pleading for these young men, interceding with her Son for these lost children of hers?

In the light of these considerations, the content of the chapel is transformed and renewed. It is not the statue of Night which is the ideal center of the work, as has been said and written for four centuries, but rather the Madonna.

Let us stand near the entrance, under the statue of the Virgin, and look around.

The priest, facing us in prayer, turns toward the Madonna. Lorenzo and Giuliano do not gaze at the altar but in the opposite direction, at the Madonna. Their guardian saints, with the gestures of their arms and heads, are beseeching the Madonna; and she, with an expression of unutterable grief and melancholy, gazes downward into the void, her head bent slightly forward, while her infant son heedlessly turns toward her breast.

Everything that is living in the chapel, or symbolically alive, from the priest to the dukes to the saints, converges on the Madonna. And she, overwhelmed but merciful, leaves all these questions in suspense. The atmosphere is that of a court of appeal just before the verdict. Will God respond? Will the heavens open to grace?

Extraneous to the drama, absorbed in themselves, the statues of Day and Night, of Twilight and Dawn, symbols of unending time, live their own life, abstract, absolute and indifferent, as reminder that the life of man on earth is not merely a fleeting moment but also the «forever» of damnation or redemption.

Michelangelo's chapel is the visible mirror, translated into volume and shape, of Dante's prayer of Saint Bernard:

Lady you are so great and so powerful
That he who seeks grace and does not turn to you
Thinks to fly without wings.

The solitary Florentine poet of the Middle Ages had found his interpreter at last in the solitary sculptor of the Renaissance. Separated by two centuries, Dante and Michelangelo, one through words, the other through stone, dedicate to the Virgin the same heartfelt prayer.

The mules of Via Larga

S AVONAROLA'S PREDICTION WAS to come true. The clouds of the Apocalypse were gathering over Florence. The glorious Florentine Republic was about to be overturned and destroyed. The Pope, who as Cardinal had been a good administrator of the city, turned out to be an incapable and indecisive governor of the Church.

Steering a middle course between Francis I and Charles V, he stipulated alliances with one or the other in the most inappropriate circumstances; and always lost.

In 1527 Rome was sacked by the Emperor's mercenaries, the *Lanzichenecchi*, and Clement VII found himself cut off and besieged in Castel Sant'Angelo.

When the news reached Florence the city was dismayed. The title of Magnificent was then held by a boy of 15 years old named Ippolito, the natural son of Giuliano Duke of Nemours. With him in the palace on Via Larga was another boy, swarthy and ill-favoured, the natural son of Lorenzo Duke of Urbino. These two illegitimate sons were known to the Florentines as «the mules».

Of course they were driven out of the city, which took the

chance to restore the institutions of the Republic. The Weepers, this time, were all followers of Savonarola, while the Palleschi, fearing a predictable retaliation, tried to disguise themselves among the moderates. Niccolò Capponi was elected Gonfalonier. The Councils were restored, and the Ten of War elected the Nine of the Militia. Florence prepared to defend itself, aware that the imperial armies would attack it from every side as soon as the Pope and the Emperor had been reconciled for the hundredth time. The city had to be fortified at once, and for this purpose an expert architect was needed: Michelangelo. The Ten of War elected him from among the Nine of the Militia, conferring on him the title of «Governor and General Procurator of Fortifications».

Michelangelo rose at daybreak to inspect the work. He had the bricks prepared with special shock-proof techniques, mixing the clay with tow and horse dung. The walls were erected in a double row, the gap between them being filled with packed earth. He had the towers «decapitated» to prevent damage resulting from their collapsing under artillery fire. He reinforced the bell tower of San Miniato and installed a mortar in it.

Meanwhile the Florentines, with great courage, laid waste the countryside around the city. Villas, monasteries, churches, castles and houses beyond the walls were demolished to leave no shelter for the enemy. Frequently it was the owners themselves who supervised this destruction, leaving the mercenaries of Charles V to find only a wasteland.

The convent erected by the Magnificent outside of the San Gallo Gate – which had lent its name to its builder Giuliano – was destroyed, as well as the convent near the Pinti Gate with all of its paintings by Perugino, and the monastery of San Salvi, beyond the Giustizia gate, where only the refectory was left standing since the demolishers could not bring themselves to ruin the splendid Last Supper just finished by the young Andrea del Sarto.

In the meantime Michelangelo had presented a fortification project that did not win the approval of the Gonfalonier Niccolò Capponi. The sculptor was advised to go to Ferrara and examine the works of Duke Alfonso d'Este. He was received there with all honors, the Duke in person accompanying him around the walls to inspect the installations. When it was time for him to leave the Duke said: «Messer Michelangelo, you are my prisoner. And I will set you free only if you promise me one of your works, either sculpture or painting, large or small, as you please». Michelangelo promised to pay that ransom and returned to Florence.

Now Francesco Carducci had been elected Gonfalonier, taking the place of Capponi. The artist resumed his post at the defense of the city, introducing the innovations suggested to him by the Duke of Ferrara. But he was concerned over the suspicious behavior of Malatesta Baglioni, whom he judged ambiguous and unfaithful to the Republic. Michelangelo went to the Gonfalonier and poured forth his doubts.

«This Michelangelo may be a great sculptor, but for me he is too suspicious and fearful», Carducci announced in public.

The sculptor, more worried every day, was working on the bastions of San Niccolò one morning when he was approached by a stranger who followed him everywhere, speaking to him continuously and greatly frightening him. The stranger went home with him, dined with him and, when night fell, convinced him to leave Florence.

With the authority of his position as Governor of Fortifications Michelangelo had one of the gates opened and, accompanied by the stranger and by his disciple Antonio Mini, left for Venice. It was September of 1529.

What was the real reason? Perhaps a plot devised by his enemies to exclude him from the defense of the city; or a proof of Baglioni's betrayal, or the fantasy of a visionary, like that of Cardiere which had caused him to abandon the palace on Via Larga so many years ago. Michelangelo never revealed the answer. From Venice, perhaps repenting of having deserted his post, he wrote to a friend to inform him of the event: «...Tuesday morning, on the twenty-first of September, came one outside the Gate of San Niccolò, where I was at the bastions, and in my ear he whispered that I should stay no longer, if I wanted to save my life. He came home with me and dined there and rode out with me, and never left me, until he brought me out of Florence, showing me that it was for my good. Either God or the devil, what he was I know not».

The Signoria banned him; but at the same time sent to call him back, granting him a safe conduct. All his Florentine friends wrote him, begging him to return. And in November he came back.

Surrounded on every side, famished, with the plague that for over a year had sewn the seeds of death in every house (Buonarroto too had died of it in Michelangelo's arms), Florence prepared for its last desperate defense.

Clement VII, reconciled with Charles V, rejected Florence's request to safeguard its Republican institutions, but tried to save his city from the horrors of being sacked.

The Emperor's Spanish troops, camped on the hills, kept the city under continuous artillery fire. Famine, plague and bombarding had depopulated the houses. Over 44,000 dead were counted. Corpses lay everywhere, on the walls, on the roofs, in the streets. Yet the resistance of the Florentines did not weaken, nor did they lose heart. The younger members of the leading families went out to every quarter to read in the parish churches the «oration to the militia»: Luigi Ala-manni in Santa Croce, Pier Filippo Pandolfini in San Loren-zo, Bartolomeo Cavalcanti in Santo Spirito, Pier Vettori in Santa Maria Novella, and Filippo Pandolfini in San Giovan-ni. These same youths, recounts Varchi, «so as not to inter-rupt the ancient custom of playing each year at football in Carnival time, and even more as greater insult to the enemies, held a game in costume in Piazza Santa Croce, twenty-five whites and twenty-five greens, with a calf as prize. And to be not merely heard, but also seen, they put musicians, with trumpets and other instruments, on the chimney-pot of the roof of Santa Croce».

In Spring of 1530, exhausted by plague and famine, Florence was forced to negotiate. Its ambassadors managed to obtain the assurance that the enemy army could not enter the walls, that the city's militia would not be disarmed and dissolved, and that the freedom of the Republic would be safeguarded. In return they promised to pay eight thousand gold florins. In the name of liberty itself, the Signoria was deposed and another was elect-ed in its place. Many heads fell. In the first days of the man-hunt Michelangelo hid out in the bell tower of San Niccolò. His enemies wanted to imprison him in the Bargello, and his house in Via Mozza was searched several times.

Very soon however, the first resentment having cooled, there came from the Pope an order not to molest the sculp-tor; on the contrary, to put him back to work at once. One of the young «mules», Alessandro, also called *Il Moro* for his dark skin, returned to Florence and was appointed Gon-falonier for life. The other, Ippolito, elected Cardinal, died soon after, a victim of poisoning.

Michelangelo dedicated himself entirely to the New Sac-risty and the Library of San Lorenzo – today the Laurentian Library – where the Pope wished to conserve all of the illu-

121

minated manuscripts that had been collected by Cosimo and by Lorenzo the Magnificent, and then laboriously retrieved all over Europe, after the palace had been sacked, by his cousin and predecessor Leo X.

Michelangelo had not, however, forgotten his debt to the Duke of Ferrara. Already during the siege he had begun for him a painting depicting Leda embracing the swan, a totally new subject for Michelangelo. After the siege of Florence Alfonso d'Este was informed that the work was finished, and sent a gentlemen of his court to get the picture. Unfortunately, that messenger was conceited and incompetent.

«Is this it? Nothing more?», exclaimed the disappointed gentleman from Ferrara.

«What trade are you in?», demanded Michelangelo.

The gentlemen, offended by this question that shed doubt on his nobility, answered sarcastically:

«If I am in Florence, what other tradesman could I be if not a merchant?».

«Well then», replied Michelangelo, «you have struck a bad bargain for your patron. Get out!», and shoved him out the door.

Having vented his anger Michelangelo gave the painting to his disciple Antonio Mini. The Leda ended up in France, at the court of King Francis I, but today its fate is unknown.

Meanwhile the heirs of Julius II continued to demand that Michelangelo account for the work on the tomb and the money paid him. Clement VII, going so far as to issue a Papal brief, helped the artist to resolve the tragedy of that sepulchre.

The parties were convened to meet in Rome, and a less demanding agreement was reached.

«But, my dear, you must make something else».

«That's what I'm doing now; the Sacristy that Your Holiness commissioned of me and the Library of San Lorenzo».

«No, Michelangelo. I am referring to something else. Aren't you the one who painted the vault of the Sistine Chapel? Well, in that chapel a great wall above the altar is waiting».

«Holy Father, waiting for what?»

«For you to paint the day of Judgement. Think about it for now. There's no hurry. When you have finished the work in San Lorenzo we will speak of it again».

On his way back to Florence Michelangelo stopped at Orvieto, as he so often did. In the Duomo was that *Last Judgement* by Luca Signorelli that he loved so much. In that fresco, a redeemed soul raised his right hand in a gesture that seemed one of irrevocable justice. He gazed long at it, and at the angels sounding the trumpets of the supreme hour, before taking again the road that led homeward.

In Florence the little tyrant Alessandro was domineering over the city, and old Lodovico was dying.

With the death of his father Michelangelo suddenly felt there was nothing more to hold him in Florence, which had now become the shadow of its former self.

PART THREE

The Pope's desire

As Michelangelo locked the door of his house in Via Mozza on that September morning he could not know that he would never return. Some obscure foreboding may have made him pause to take one last look at his belongings – books, scattered sheets of paper, projects, drawings, the statue of Victory already finished, the captives barely roughed out. But outside the faithful Urbino was waiting with the stamping horses and the clear air of September, sparkling after the late August storms, was an invitation to depart.

Michelangelo intended to go to Rome to finish the tomb of Julius II and stay there as long as necessary. He would be far from Florence, where the arrogant Alessandro, to whom he had refused to give advice and service, was awaiting his chance for revenge.

Instead of the Via Cassia Michelangelo took the road for Pescia and Pisa, traveling along the Via Aurelia to arrive in Rome on September 27, 1534. He found the city in mourning. Clement VII had died two days before.

«That was a narrow escape», exclaimed the young Urbino. «If we were still waiting to leave, we would have left all right, but for the other world. Now, without his Uncle the Pope, Il Moro will show no respect for anyone».

Michelangelo sighed in silent agreement. With Clement he had lost his last friend in the Medici family and the last survivor of that brief happy time in Via Larga.

He found again the first cartoons for the *Last Judgement*. He had made them for Clement, during brief stays in Rome, well knowing that the Pope would soon bring up this subject again. If he were still alive, Clement would already have put him to work in Pope Sixtus' chapel. With Leo X, a son, and Clement VII, a grandson, the magnificence of Lorenzo de' Medici had now come to an end. But the grandson of the Magnificent had triumphantly concluded a glorious family tradition by commissioning of Michelangelo the *Last Judgement* and of Machiavelli the *Florentine Histories*.

«Enough, Urbino», said Michelangelo to his pupil, «now this work will not be done and we can dedicate all our time to the tomb of Pope Julius».

The statue of Moses, almost finished, needed only the last touches. Two figures of women, Lia and Rachel, barely roughed out, still had to emerge from the marble.

In Florence Michelangelo had devised a simple, rudimentary system for transferring the proportions of his wax models to the marble. While working on the statues in the Chapel of San Lorenzo he had devised a scheme for immersing the model in water and then, by gradually decreasing the level of the liquid, transferring the various planes to the marble. To do this, he put the wax model in a box filled with water, then let the water trickle out through a hole. Gradually, a knee emerged, then a shoulder, then the nose. In this way, working on the marble and starting from an ideal plane corresponding to the surface of the fluid, the artist knew where and when the different planes of the work should appear in the marble. Then by gradually decreasing the level of the water, he found them all again until the entire figure was freed from the surface that surrounded it.

Urbino was just preparing a box like the one Michelangelo had used in Florence when a messenger from the Pope arrived. His Holiness Paul III wanted to see the sculptor immediately.

Alessandro Farnese, crowned Pope on November 5, 1534 under the name of Paul III, had wasted no time in calling for him. Michelangelo protested that he had promised the Duke of Urbino to finish the tomb of Julius II, but the Reformation Pope, energetic and decided, answered him:

«Michelangelo, for thirty years I have wanted you to work for me. And now that I am Pope, shouldn't I satisfy this desire? Where is the contract with the Duke of Urbino, I want to tear it up!».

The sculptor returned home in distress. This Pope, like the Della Rovere one, threatened to have his way at all costs.

«I'll go away, near Genoa», Michelangelo told Urbino. «The bishop of Aleria is a good friend of mine, and Carrara is not far. I could quarry the marble with no problems. Or I could go to Urbino, it's a quiet place and they will welcome me there to finish the tomb of Pope Julius».

But his words did not ring with conviction. Michelangelo knew men, and he had realized at once that the Farnese Pope would use any means, including prison, to keep him in Rome.

He had been torn by these thoughts for some days when one morning a knock was heard at the door.

It was the Pope, accompanied by a group of Cardinals, who wanted to have a look at Michelangelo's work.

«What are these things?»

«Your Holiness, they are the cartoons for the *Judgement*».

«What *Judgement*?»

«The Last Judgement that Pope Clement wanted me to make on the wall above the altar in Pope Sixtus' chapel».

Paul III examined the cartoons closely, at length, and was struck by them.

In a corner stood the statue of Moses, almost finished. A cardinal remarked, «But this statue alone is more than enough to honor the sepulchre of Pope Julius».

Paul III, now burning with the desire to have Michelangelo paint the *Judgement*, added:

«I will see that the Duke of Urbino is satisfied with three statues from your hand, and the other three will be made by others».

On returning to his palace the Pope immediately issued a brief in which he appointed Michelangelo «supreme architect, sculptor and painter of the apostolic palace», enrolling him among his followers and reconfirming his lifetime annuity of 1200 gold *scudi* a year. A little later the Duke of Urbino wrote him, declaring himself willing «... to support with good patience your subsequent involvement in that work, while His Holiness keeps you occupied in painting the chapel known as that of Sixtus...».

So Michelangelo returned to the chapel that had once been the scene of his dramatic isolation and his first inhuman, or rather superhuman, contact with wall painting.

The testimony was there, in the vault peopled by characters, in those figures issued not from his hands alone, but from his heart and his thought.

In a year he completed all of the cartoons, erected a solid scaffolding with the help of Urbino, carefully prepared the wall with the first plaster and finally began the fresco.

It was the Spring of 1536. Almost six years later, on Christmas Eve, a solemn mass consecrated the unveiling of the wall, rendering manifest *urbi et orbi* the day of the *Last Judgement*.

The flayed skin

DANTE AND THE Apocalypse: these are the great abiding spirits and the sublime components of the *Judgement*. Seven angels sound the terrifying trumpets of the last hour, graves gape open, the dead rise again. Charon's ferry is packed with the damned, while demons clutch at the naked bodies to drag them down into the whirlpool of damnation. The proud, the heretics, the betrayers, all are seized and overwhelmed. Men and women fall into the abyss without light and without shores, while the redeemed gather around Christ. And He, no longer the messenger of peace and prince of love, is the supreme judge, awful and terrifying. His right hand is raised high to decree salvation or irrevocable damnation.

Around Christ the crowd of saints is dense and compact. The Madonna turns aside in distress, with maternal sympathy for the common anguish. Above Christ a group of angels, on the left, overturns a cross, symbol of martyrdom and humiliation, while another group on the right throws down a column, symbol of earthly and temporal power.

Humanity, surprised by the hour of darkness, is shown in a moment of convulsion, naked without and within. Each figure reveals its inner drama in a particular gesture of its own, its individuality heightened by the diversity of anatomical details.

The supremely skillful use of foreshortening, light and shadow confers on the painting an almost three-dimensional effect.

«... I see amidst the turmoil the Antichrist, with a countenance conceived only by you. I see the fright in the faces of the living. I see the sun, the moon and the stars as their light goes out. I see the spirit of fire, air, earth and water almost extinguishing. I see, standing apart, dismayed Nature, sterile in her decrepit age. I see Time dry and trembling, who, having reached his end, is seated on a dry throne. And while I hear from the trumpets of the angels shaking the hearts in all the breasts, I see Life, Death oppressed by horrible confusion.... I see the ministers of the abyss... I see Fame with her crowns... and lastly I see issuing from the mouth of the Son of God the great sentence...».

These are the words of the ambitious Aretino. Knowing like everyone else in Italy that Michelangelo was working on a great painting of the *Judgement Day*, he was offering suggestions on how it should be done, in the attempt to link his dubious reputation with the artist's clear fame.

In his rhetoric Aretino goes so far as to describe the details: only the color scheme is missing.

But Michelangelo took no heed. Aretino's letter was written in 1537, and by then the artist had gone so far with his work that he could kindly decline the offer.

«... On receiving your letter I have felt joy and grief together. I rejoiced greatly because it came from you who, a man of unique talent; but I am very regretful because, having completed a great part of the composition, I cannot put into my work what you have imagined...». But Michelangelo committed the mistake of promising Aretino one of his works, and then forgetting the promise. And Aretino was not to forget this offense.

Sometimes Paul III came to see him. He too, like Julius II, loved to follow the different stages of the painting, observing its progress. One day he visited Michelangelo accompanied by Biagio da Cesena, master of ceremonies.

«Biagio, what do you think of these figures?», demanded the Pope.

«Your Holiness will pardon me, but to me they seem not

merely dishonest, but extremely dishonest. All those nudes, without even a veil to cover their private parts, are more suitable to a house of sin than to a Chapel».

The Pope did not reply. But when they had gone Michelangelo, boiling with rage, took up his brush and painted the devil Minos with the face of the scandalized master of ceremonies.

When Biagio da Cesena heard about it he went to the Pope to protest.

«My dear Biagio, if Michelangelo had put you in Purgatory, I would have made every effort to help you; but since he has placed you in Hell, it is useless for you to appeal to me, because there *nulla est redemptio*». And in fact Minos is still there, wearing the frowning face of the master of ceremonies.

Along with that image are others however, evoked by memory and by love; Dante, his great fellow citizen, and Savonarola; Julius II, Clement VII, and Paul III.

The face of the Madonna is clearly that of Vittoria Colonna, the woman he loved.

Aretino is represented in San Bartholomew who died of flaying, the skin pulled off his body like a glove. Standing among the redeemed, he holds out to Christ the knife, instrument of his torture, while over his other arm hangs like a rag the skin that has been flayed from him. In the folds of the skin can be seen a desperate, tragically deformed face: that of Michelangelo.

«Call Messer Tommaso de' Cavalieri, or Messer Donato Giannotti, or His Holiness! Michelangelo is ill!».

Urbino, unable to leave the house, was calling for help from the window.

Three days before his master had fallen from the scaffolding and injured his leg. Instead of calling a doctor he had

had himself carried home, ordering that the door be locked and no one allowed to enter.

His friends immediately notified Baccio Rontini, Michelangelo's doctor, who went to the house in Macel de' Corvi.

The door was locked even to him, so entering another house and passing from one balcony to another, Master Baccio came into Michelangelo's bedroom through the window. He found the artist desperately ill. Patiently he cut off his boot, removing the stocking that was attached to the skin and the skin itself that came away like a shell. Then he medicated the wounds and stayed with Michelangelo until he was well again.

This time too, like thirty years before, Michelangelo had forgotten himself, totally absorbed in his painting.

«Often he ate only a piece of bread», recounts his biographer, «without stopping work».

He slept without undressing, on the scaffolding or at home, and without ever removing his boots because he «suffered from cramps». On the rare occasions when he did try to take them off he had to exert great effort, so that the skin came away with the boots «like that of a serpent».

Three years for the vault, six years for the wall; the beginning and end of life; the paternal right hand of Jehovah waking Adam from his sleep of stone, the mighty right hand of Christ waking the dead to judgement.

The second vision is more Dantesque, and more tragic; just as the artist was now more tragic and alone.

Two friendships

TWO THINGS, OR better, two persons had drawn Michelangelo from Florence to Rome with the silent eloquence of feeling: a young man from the de' Cavalieri family, and the Marchioness of Pescara. Two loves.

Tommaso de' Cavalieri had appeared to Michelangelo as the personification of that classical ideal of beauty which, for the Greeks, existed in the demigod. Vittoria Colonna had inspired in him a more romantic feeling, nourished by a perfect spiritual kinship.

Of course there was malignant gossip about both of these friendships. Michelangelo replied only by dignified silence.

Undoubtedly, his affection for the young Roman was very strong. Ill-favored in face and aspect himself, Michelangelo was fired with admiration for that young demigod. The learned discussions of his humanist masters had prepared him for this event. The Platonic idea had finally descended to the realm of real life, incarnate in an individual.

The old sculptor addressed young Tommaso in carefully-chosen words, even re-writing the same letter twice to express in the best literary form his «very great, even immeasurable love». He gave Tommaso painting lessons, drew for him the heads of gods, cartoons on mythological subjects, and beautifully detailed anatomical tables.

Tommaso Cavalieri replied to these letters with respect and veneration, showing Michelangelo his profound gratitude at the unexpected fortune of having him as maestro.

«I can only write you to come back soon, because in coming back you will free me from prison, since I flee bad company and, desiring to flee it, I can stay with no other than you».

And Michelangelo returned to Rome. During the rare pauses in his work he continued to meet his young friend, happy to converse with him, watching over his work and his life with paternal affection.

With Vittoria Colonna instead, friendship gradually matured into tender emotion and even more into profound mutual admiration. Vittoria was forty-five years old when she met Michelangelo and he was about sixty. Left the widow of Ferrante d'Avalos, Marquis of Pescara, at an early age, she had wanted to become a nun, but the Pope had convinced her not to take the veil while granting her permission to live in a convent. She had chosen that of San Silvestro, in Viterbo. She was famous both for her poetry and as a woman versed in religious doctrine.

In an age when the Christian religion was exploited for exclusively temporal aims, she gathered about her a group of spirits less indulgent toward the Curia, and even protected those who dared to show open dissent.

Her circle of friends included authoritative sympathizers with Luther, such as Bernardino Ochino, Sadoleto, Giberti, Carafa, Thiene, and Pole. Formed in the school of Giovanni Valdès, who had brought to Italy the message of Luther and Erasmus, these clergymen had moved from Rome to Viterbo. Vittoria Colonna, with the authority of her rank and fame, immediately became the leader and protector of the group.

Michelangelo participated in these meetings. He too was familiar with the basic lines of Luther's dissent. In the words of the German Agostinian monk he heard the ardent echo of Savonarola's preachings. Luther maintained that salvation depended on faith, not good works; and grace was linked to faith, not actions.

But Paul III could not allow men of deep theological learning and exemplary lives, such as the friends of the Marchioness of Pescara, to become not merely sympathizers but supporters of the *protest*. He called the most authoritative of them, such as Sadoleto, Thiene, and Carafa, to participate in the special committee *de renovanda Ecclesia*.

Ochino instead went over to the Protestants, and the group broke up.

Michelangelo remained faithful to Vittoria Colonna, along with Cardinal Reginald Pole, her spiritual director.

Each day, in the Sistine Chapel, the artist had before his eyes the dramatic vision and the tragic question of salvation. He could condemn or redeem his personages, evoking in their aid either faith or good works. He could and must respond to himself, to his inner strife.

«Messer Michelangelo, I understand your conflict, because it is mine as well», Vittoria Colonna told him one day, «but we must not forget the words of the Apostle Paul, when he says that faith without charity is nothing».

«But my lady Marchioness, charity is love, and love always shows itself in good works».

«Precisely. And we, although we are still alone to declare it, we must believe as if salvation depended only on our faith, and act as if salvation depended only on our actions».

Michelangelo listened and assented, immediately agreeing with those words. No one, before this extraordinary woman, had ever read the secrets in his heart, responding to his inner thoughts, lovingly resolving his doubts.

For her Michelangelo rediscovered poetry. From Florence he had already written sonnets and other compositions to his young friend Tommaso, but Vittoria suddenly reawakened his inspiration and the verses flowed effortlessly from the old sculptor's loving pen. They were poems overflowing with admiration, where the spirit of Petrarch guided the author's hand, and hyperbole led the language to such refinement that the figure of the beloved woman could hardly be distinguished from that of the Madonna.

And with the Virgin he purposely identified the Marchioness of Pescara, in the face and the emotion of the Madonna in the *Last Judgement*.

He made for her a Crucifix, a Pietà, a Samaritan, magnificent works, report his biographers, lost to us today. Michelangelo expressed his love with all the means he possessed, and Vittoria responded with warm affection, giving him all of her poems, writing him affectionate letters, purposely not replying to his poems in verse so that their correspondence would not be mere literature.

«Magnificent Messer Michel Agnolo,

I have not answered your letter before because it was, we may say, a reply to mine, thinking that, if you and I continue to write according to my obligation and your courtesy, I will be obliged to leave the Chapel of Saint Catherine, no longer finding myself at the appointed hour in the company of these nuns, and you will leave the Chapel of Saint Paul without finding yourself all day, from before dawn, in the gentle converse of your paintings...».

In other words, with feminine grace, Vittoria clearly pointed out their respective plights, disclosing the feeling that united them, for which he would willing have ceased to paint and she to pray, «...so that I to the brides and you to the Vicar of Christ will be failing».

But by now Vittoria could no longer stay in Viterbo, and decided to return definitively to Rome. There she visited him often to watch him work, and waited for him in the Benedictine monastery of Sant'Anna, where a group of friends gathered to speak of religion, art and poetry.

A Portuguese painter, Francisco de Hollanda, has left a book of memoirs on those conversations between Michelangelo, the Marchioness of Pescara and Lattanzio Tolomei.

«..I saw her», writes Francisco, «act as he who, armed with

stratagems and circumspection, sets out to vanquish an unconquerable fortress. And in the same way, I saw Michelangelo attentive and vigilant, as if he were besieged...But it was the Marchioness who was victorious, in the end. And truly I do not know who could have resisted...».

Michelangelo, once the ice had been broken, spoke clearly and sincerely. To his friend he said one day: «I have to say that even His Holiness sometimes annoys me and importunes me, when he insistently asks me why I do not go to see him more often. But to serve the Pope there is no need that I run at his every call, seeking in this way my interest, but rather that I stay at home and do my best».

«But a prince who was not pope, would he pardon such a sin?», asked the Portuguese painter.

«Sins of this kind, Messer Francisco, are precisely those that sovereigns should pardon», replied Michelangelo with a smile.

Then he added, «I must tell you that my great calling at times gives me such license that, while I am speaking with the Pope, I use with him maximum frankness and thoughtlessly I put my felt hat on my head...».

Vittoria provoked him lovingly, and he responded with devoted obedience.

«Let Your Excellency only ask me one thing that I can give her, and it will be hers». Then, returning home, he wrote her verses, sending them to her next day accompanied by a note or a drawing.

> *A man in a woman, nay a God*
> *Through her mouth speaks,*
> *Where I to hear her*
> *Am so made that never more will I be mine....*

«Lasting friendship, bound by a Christian knot in most sure affection», was the poetess' definition of the feeling that united them.

But for the sculptor it was even more. Having lived for sixty years melancholy and alone, that friendship was the first warm presence to which he willingly surrendered.

The biographer's words ring with truth when he reports that Michelangelo «so great love did he feel for her that I remember hearing him say that his only regret was that, on going to see her when she was dying, he did not kiss her on the forehead or the face but kissed instead her hand. For her death he seemed at times stunned, almost insensate».

It was February of 1547. Vittoria was fifty-six years old, Michelangelo seventy-two.

Il Braghettone

THE UNVEILING OF the *Last Judgement* was greeted with an almost unanimous chorus of protest. What is surprising today is the attitude of the Pope, who showed more understanding for Michelangelo that agreement with his reverend censors. That assembly of nudes was a scandal without precedent, especially in a papal chapel.

Even a libellist such as Aretino, who lived on the income from obscenity, became the champion of the general hypocrisy, writing Michelangelo a letter as indignant as it was insincere:

«...Is it possible that you, so divine that you do not deign to consort with men, have done such a thing in the highest temple of God? above the first altar of Jesus? Not even in the brothel are there such scenes as yours; and it were better for you and for art if you had followed my suggestion».

This was the point. Aretino was offended because Michelangelo had not taken his emphatic letter seriously, and because he had not sent him, as promised, one of his works.

Aretino was echoed by the reformist friar Bernardino Ochino, then by Ludovico Dolce, an expert in painting. There was pasquinades and epigrams against the Pope who tolerated such an insult to modesty in the house of God.

The uproar continued unabated, like a word of order from the theologians and the cardinals in the Curia, until twenty years later when the outraged prudes won their point.

In 1564, slightly before Michelangelo died, Pope Pius IV decreed that those nudes should be decently covered. The work was assigned to a painter who was a friend of Michelangelo's, Daniele da Volterra, who added veils and drapery over the «shameful parts», shadowing and shading, until the censors could breathe a sigh of relief. The *Last Judgement* changed aspect and color. The saints, like the damned, were dressed in «pants», and poor Master Daniele, to his misfortune, has gone done in history as «Il Braghettone», the pants-maker.

But one of Michelangelo's young pupils, Marcello Venuti from Como, had diligently copied the fresco before it was covered. The copy is now in the Naples Museum, and it gives a good idea of the original and of the damage wrought by time and the hand of man.

Michelangelo, having finished the fresco of the *Last Judgement*, had resumed work on the statues for the tomb of Julius II.

But Paul III had other things in mind for him, and summoned him to paint the chapel that Antonio da Sangallo had just completed.

«The desire that this chapel too be embellished and decorated by the painting of Michelangelo came naturally to the Pope. Therefore, with his authority and the very great love he bore him, he exhorted him many times and with many words».

After having begun the first fresco in the Pauline Chapel, Michelangelo began to realize that even the new agreement with the Duke of Urbino, for the tomb of Julius II, was a burden to him. Age no longer allowed him to make promises without the risk of being unable to keep them. The commitment to make two other statues, in addition to that of Moses, literally paralyzed his energy. And now again the Pope was interfering in the question, getting the heir of Julius II to agree that Michelangelo would have to furnish only the statue of Moses, while the other two statues, Lia and Rachel, would be designed by him but sculpted by artists of his choice.

Michelangelo paid one thousand four hundred *scudi* to those who had worked, or were still to work, on the tomb, namely his assistant Urbino, Raffaello da Montelupo and Giovanni de' Marchesi. And finally, on August 22, 1542, the long tragedy of the Della Rovere Pope's tomb concluded with an agreement in writing that absolved Michelangelo from any obligation or promise.

Relieved in body and soul, the artist could resume in the Pauline Chapel that «sweet converse with his paintings» of which Vittoria Colonna had spoken. There were two great panels, one representing the conversion of Saint Paul on the road to Damascus, the other the crucifixion of Saint Peter. But these were not the only commitments of the aging Michelangelo. He supervised the installation of the tomb of Julius II in San Peter's Ad Vinculum. He assumed responsibility, again at the desire of the Pope, for the fortifications of Rome and the cornice of Palazzo Farnese. In collaboration with Tommaso de' Cavalieri he drew up a project for Piazza del Campidoglio. Lastly, as if all this were not enough, he was appointed architect of the Fabric of Saint Peter's.

The frescos in the Pauline Chapel reflect this fatigue, although the imprint of the lion's paw, the unmistakable mark of his genius, is still clearly apparent.

First he painted the fresco of the conversion of Paul, dividing it into two parts, the heavenly population and the earthly one. God, accompanied by his angels, behind the symbol of light, stretches out his arm and his whole body toward the earth, where the followers of Paul succor the apostle, blinded by the dazzling vision and fallen from his horse. Nude or dressed, the bodies are all in motion. The horse is riderless. Paul, lying on the ground, is stunned. The figures behind him, especially those in profile, seem to issue from the congregation of the blessed in the *Last Judgement*.

In the background is a landscape – rare in Michelangelo's work – with a mysterious city, an imaginary Damascus, half-hidden among the hills.

The other fresco shows the crucifixion of Peter, at the moment when the old apostle, in a spasmodic contortion of his body, lifts his head to look backwards. His gaze is the real and ideal center of the whole composition. Under the cross is a crouching figure, foreshortened, depicted with the same sculptural characteristics as some of the damned in the Sistine Chapel. Each countenance expresses a different sentiment. A man with a sad, hooded face, his arms crossed, standing at the extreme right of the fresco, is probably a melancholy self-portrait.

These were the artist's last two paintings, and they cost him, as he himself confessed, «very great fatigue, since painting, having passed a certain age, and to a maximum degree working in fresco, is not an art for old men».

He had to stop work frequently to recover enough energy to go on. His friends rejoiced at these forced pauses, at the chance to have him among them again. These friends were called Tommaso de' Cavalieri, Luigi del Riccio, Claudio Tolomei, Lionardo Malespini, Donato Giannotti, Realdo Colombo, Lorenzo Ridolfi, Antonio Petreo, and, of course, Vittoria Colonna. One evening Giannotti and Michelangelo, descending from the Campidoglio, met Riccio and Petreo. They walked on together, glad to have met, and began to speak of Dante. All were anxious to hear Michelangelo's opinion, since his fame as a student of Dante was wide-spread among the Florentine exiles. The question debated that evening was how many days Dante had taken in searching for Hell and Purgatory.

Two days, as stated by the humanist Cristoforo Landino in his famous comment on the *Divine Comedy*, or three natural days as Petreo maintained instead?

At the end of the discussion, reports Donato Giannotti, Luigi del Riccio proposed that they dine together. This dialogue deserves to be reported, for the extraordinary statements made by Michelangelo.

Luigi (del Riccio): «The best thing that you could do, would be that you all come to dinner with me».

Antonio (Petreo): «If Messer Michelangelo would come, we could all come very willingly».

Michelangelo: «I don't promise you I will come».

Luigi: «Why?»

Michelangelo: «Because I want to stay by myself».

Luigi: «For what reason?»

Michelangelo: «Because when I find myself in one of these brigades, as would happen if I dined with you, I rejoice too much; and I do not want to rejoice over much».

Luigi: «Oh, this is the newest thing I every heard! Who is it that, to recompense in part the worry and suffering and cares that plague him in this life, does not search for some joy at times, some merriment; for which he, forgetful of everything that is heavy and annoying to him, seems to find himself again and enjoys it greatly? ...Come then to dine with us. Here there will be only virtuous and affectionate persons, by whom you will be greatly loved and desired... And I promise you, if you come, that we will all dance, to chase the melancholy from your soul».

Michelangelo: «Oh you make me laugh, that you want to dance. I tell you that in this world there is that to make us weep».

Luigi: «But we must laugh, to conserve ourselves as well as we can; and to this Nature invites us».

Michelangelo: «You are in great error. And to show you that you have given yourself, as we saw, a blow on the foot with this reasoning of yours that you have expressed to persuade me to dine with you, know that I am the man most inclined to love persons, that ever in any time was born. Whenever I see anyone who has some virtue, who shows some skill, who knows how to do or say something better than others, I am obliged to fall in love with him; and I am so taken with him that I am no longer mine, but all his.

«If then I were to dine with you, all of you being adorned with virtues and courtesy, in addition to what each of you three has robbed of me here, each of those who dined with us would take a part of me. One part of me would be taken by the musician; another by he who danced; and each of the others would have his part. So that I, thinking by rejoicing with you to find myself again, as you were saying, would entirely surrender myself and be lost; so that for many days I would not know in what world I was».

The group of friends continued to meet, and Dante was often the subject of their discussions. One day the theme of the conversation was both poetical and political: Brutus and Cassius. Why had they been put in the reign of Lucifer? Didn't Dante know that Caesar was a tyrant? Brutus and Cassius should have been rewarded and praised, not condemned.

Only a few years earlier, in 1537, Duke Alessandro de' Medici had been murdered by his cousin Lorenzino, who had then fled Florence proclaiming himself a new Brutus. The government of the city had been offered to the very young Cosimo, the son of Giovanni dalle Bande Nere, who had quickly shown himself to be tougher and more astute than his predecessor.

The Florentine exiles who were Michelangelo's friends accused Dante of conniving with Caesar in the name of that freedom which another Caesar, of much lower stature, had stolen from them and their homeland.

«How do you know whether Dante thought that Brutus and Cassius did ill to kill Caesar?», interjected Michelangelo. «Don't you know how much ruin was brought into the world by the death of that man?».

«But Brutus and Cassius knew that Caesar wanted to become king».

«Yes. But who knows whether Caesar, becoming in time satiated with dominion, might not have done as Sylla did, and given back freedom to his land?... It is a great presumption to decide to kill a prince, just or unjust as he may be, not knowing with certainty what good may come from his death. I find heavy and dull those who think that good must start with evil, that is with deaths...».

The conversation went on, concluding in the full absolution of Dante and the reading of a sonnet to him written by Michelangelo.

These friendly disputes that took place in the evening, strolling through the lonely tree-lined streets of Rome, refreshed Michelangelo's spirit, lightened the burden of the work that had now become hard labor. Music too helped to lift his morale, especially when his friends sang his own madrigals put to music by Archadelt or by the Veronese composer Bartolomeo Tromboncino.

«Have you heard», said Donato Giannotti one evening to his friends, «the news that Lorenzino de' Medici has been murdered in Venice? The hand of Cosimo is long and pitiless».

Among the group was Niccolò Ridolfi, grandson of the Magnificent and son of the gentle Contessina, who had gone as bride slightly before Michelangelo left the palace in Via Larga forever.

«Monsignor», continued Giannotti, «why not ask Michelangelo for a portrait of Lorenzino? He will not make it a likeness. He may not even want to do it. But you could ask him for a bust of Brutus, according to his fantasy».

Michelangelo loved Contessina's son, who reminded him of his long-ago, almost mythological boyhood, and of the melancholic countenance of Lorenzo's youngest daughter, of the revered secret of a first sentiment. And the head of Brutus, apparently unfinished but alive and speaking in its proud expression, is now in the Bargello Museum in Florence, testifying through the centuries to the Florentine exiles' ardent love of freedom.

Imperial blood

«LIONARDO, I SENT you in my last letter a note of several eligible girls, which was sent me by someone, some marriage broker, I believe. ... I believe that there are in Florence many noble and poor families, that it would be an act of charity to marry with, where there is no dowry, because then there would be no haughtiness... Not that you need to seek nobility, because it is known that we are ancient citizens of Florence and noble above all else...».

To what ancient nobility was Michelangelo referring?

«Lionardo... in the book of contracts there is a letter from Count Alessandro di Canossa that I found at home..., who came to visit me in Rome as a relative. Take heed of it».

In 1520, in fact, a certain Count Alessandro di Canossa had written to the already famous sculptor calling him «honorable relative» and inviting him to visit «to know your family and your home». In the same letter the Count explained to Michelangelo the reasons for their kinship. «Searching in our ancient things I have found a certain Messer Simone di Canossa to have been *podestà* of Florence». That Messer Simone had been the founder of the Simoni family, later to become Buonarroti-Simoni.

Michelangelo's biographer Condivi, who diligently wrote what his master told him, even speaks of imperial blood. And Michelangelo, as can be seen from the many letters written to his nephew Leonardo exhorting him to take a wife and advising him how to choose her, always stressed the nobility of his lineage.

«Choose a wife who is noble and poor», he reiterated, «not to ennoble yourself, because we have no need of it, but to have a companion worthy to bear our name and without too many flighty ideas in her head».

This letter to his nephew opens a window on the artist's life, throwing light on the lesser known aspects, revealing him in his humanity and daily life.

In Florence lived Michelangelo's two younger brothers, Giovan Simone and Sigismondo, the young Leonardo, son of the deceased Buonarroto, and his sister Francesca married to Michele Guicciardini.

«...and when you write me, do not write on the letter, *Michelagniolo Simoni,* nor *sculptor*; it is enough to say, *Michelagniol Buonarroti – Rome*».

The letters to his nephew are lively, curious, and interesting, at times resentful, almost ferocious, then paternally concerned. All of them, however, reveal a great need for sincere affection, the fear of being loved or respected in words only for the heredity he would leave, the fear of feeling himself dead in the hearts of his descendants.

«Lionardo. I have been ill. And you have come to deal me death, and to see if I am leaving anything. Don't you have enough of mine in Florence already? You cannot deny that you resemble our father, who in Florence threw me out of my own house. Know that I have made a will such that, of what I have in Rome, you can forget about it. But go with God and don't come to see me and don't write me ever again».

This letter is like the one written so many years before to his brother Giovan Simone. But while that letter was just in its noble indignation, this one was false and unfair. Michelangelo had been ill, at death's door. Luigi del Riccio had taken him into his own home, near the Strozzi palace, so that he would be better cared for. Suffering from high fever, vomit and delirium, he was so ill that his Roman friends thought they should notify his relatives in Florence. Leonardo had

149

come running. After surviving the crisis, his old uncle wrote him that letter. But this «definitive» split lasted only the time of a summer storm.

«Lionardo. I do not want to fail in that which I have been long thinking; and that is, to help you...», and he sent him two hundred gold *scudi* to be employed «in the wool merchant's guild», that is to be suitably invested.

«Lionardo. I understand by your letters that you have not yet decided where to invest the money I sent you... but I would like you to take your time and invest it anywhere, as long as you do not squander it...».

«Lionardo. I do not believe that you can keep money in any place to earn by it, that it cannot be called usury, unless it is subjected to loss as well as profit...».

This is a just consideration. Apart from usury, condemned as sin, any economic utilization of money is subject to the law of risk. Those who do not want to risk should not ask for high dividends from their capital, but be satisfied to earn a fair amount.

«Lionardo. I wrote you last Saturday that I would have preferred two flasks of wine to the eight shirts you sent me. Now I tell you how I received the barrel of wine, that is 44 bottles, of which I have sent six to the Pope and to other friends, so that I have gotten rid of almost all of them, since I cannot drink...».

It seems incredible today that Michelangelo distributed the wine among his friends, including His Holiness Paul III.

But at that time, with the Italian countryside devastated by armies constantly on the move, wine was such a rarity that it could even be offered to the Pope.

«We will drink this wine from our Michelangelo», Paul III will have said with a smile, «and then we will go to see how he is doing with those paintings in the chapel».

«Lionardo. One day when I have time, I will tell you about our origins and from where and when we came to Florence, which perhaps you do not know. But we should not lose what God has given us...».

«Lionardo. There came into my hands about a year ago a book written by the hand of Florentine chroniclers, in which I found, about two hundred years ago if I remember rightly, a Buonarroto Simoni several times member of the Signoria...».

It was an obsession: nobility in poverty, the illustrious origins of the family in spite of the humble occupations to which his father Lodovico had had to lower himself. Then again:

«Lionardo. About the other house of which you have written me, I cannot reply to the letter because I cannot understand it. I never have a letter from you that I am not struck by fever before I can read it. I don't know where you learned to write. Little love!».

Poor Leonardo; there was more scolding than tenderness. But the young man would not have taken it too seriously, he was used to it. From the letters it is obvious that Leonardo willingly accepted the advice of his grand old uncle. It was he who asked for Michelangelo's opinion on everything that concerned him, including the choice of a wife. He must have been, rather than affectionate, respectful. He feared, admired and venerated his great relative, and was proud to bear his name. Giovan Simone and Sigismondo instead replied unwillingly to the rare letters from their brother, and always through their nephew Leonardo. They obeyed, of course, since Michelangelo minced no words and knew how to make his wishes known even from afar.

«Lionardo. I have always tried to raise our family, but I have received nothing from this. However, see that you do what I am writing, and that Gismondo comes back to live in Florence, so that it cannot be said to my shame that I have a brother who goes after the oxen at Settignano».

He was attentive to the words of his nephew, pondering over them, analyzing them. And if he found a singular used in place of a plural, he wrote:

«Lionardo. I have had the receipt for the *scudi* you have received... and I have greatly marveled that Gismondo neither for these latest ones nor for the first has come to you for them, because what I sent is as much for them as for you. You write me that you thank me for the good I do you, and your write me: *we thank you for the good you do us*. With those same conditions that I wrote you... I have sent you this, namely that you do nothing without the consent of my brothers...».

Michelangelo sent his gold *scudi* to Florence, at quite regular intervals, considering that he was sending them more to his family than to its individual members; and he wanted to respect the formalities, with the due subordination of the nephew to his other uncles.

«Lionardo. I have from you the receipt for five hundred fifty gold *scudi*, as I counted here to Bettino. You write me that you would give four to that woman for the love of God. I am agreed. The rest, up to fifty, I wish that they also be given for the love of God, some for the soul of Buonarroto your father and some for mine. But try to find some needy citizen who has daughters either to be married or to be put in the convent, and give them to him, but secretly...».

There still exists in Florence the little church of the Bishop of Saint Martin's, or of the «poor and ashamed». People still leave alms there, because the poverty of the Florentines is as dignified now as in the time of Michelangelo. It may be that even old Lodovico had received from Saint Martin's, in the darkest days of his life, concrete, discreet help allowing him to go on in the hope of better days. It is certain that Michelangelo thought often of that church and of the anonymous poor who flocked to it.

«Lionardo. ...I am old as I wrote you in my last letter, and to abolish vain hopes from someone, should they exist, I am thinking to make a will and leave what I have there to Gismondo my brother and to you my nephew, stipulating that neither of you can make decisions of any sort without the consent of the other. And should you remain without legitimate heirs, everything will be left to Saint Martin's, so that the income will be given for the love of God to the shameful, that is to the poor citizens....».

Giovan Simone had died, and Michelangelo had wanted to know «what kind of death he had made, and if he had died confessed and communicated with all of the things ordered by the Church... because if he had... I would feel less passion».

Once his nephew sent him some pears and cheese. The pears arrived, but the thieving carter kept the cheese for himself.

«Lionardo. I had the pears, which were eighty-six. I sent thirty-three to the Pope. He found them beautiful and was very grateful. Of the piece of cheese, the Customs says that the carter is a bad one, and that he did not bring it into the customs office. If I find out he is in Rome I will give him what he deserves, not on account of the cheese, but to teach him to have so little respect for men...». Then in the same letter he invites his nephew to discretely inform the priest – someone who had written him from Florence requesting a religious painting – not to address him as «... *Michelagnolo sculptor* because I am known here only as Michelagniolo Buonarroti, and if a citizen of Florence wants to have an altarpiece painted, he must find a painter, for I was never painter nor sculptor like one who has a workshop. I have always kept myself from this for the honor of my father and my brothers, although I have served three Popes, and it was hard».

And what of the beatings administered by his father Lodovico to the boy who wanted to be apprenticed to Ghirlandaio? After having sculpted almost all of his statues and painted the vault and the wall of the Sistine Chapel, Michelangelo realized that his father was right to consider the profession of sculptor and painter dishonorable, because the words «sculptor» and «painter» appeared on shop signs under the name of the owner.

Health in body and soul, and a wife for Leonardo, were now the recurrent themes of the letters, spiced as usual by advice and scolding to which his young nephew probably paid little heed.

«...a girl of noble family, well brought-up and good and very poor... this would be most suitable... and I desire this very much, that you should not be dazzled by pomp and frivolity, and you should be good to others, as others have been to you. But you find yourself rich, and you know not how. I will not go into details in describing to you the poverty in which I found our family, when I began to help them. A book would not suffice to describe it; and I have never had anything but ingratitude...».

Michelangelo, like all grand old men who have built up a fortune, was a conservative, suspicious of any innovation, considering everything not strictly necessary to life to be a luxury. Those who spent his money were rebuked for not appreciating its value. Above all he feared, as in this case, that Leonard might blunder into a marriage with a rich, spend-thrift wife who would quickly squander his estate.

«...You write me that they have spoken to you of that woman and told you that I wish it very much... and I confirm it to you, so that our family will not end here», that is, to hand down the family name to future generations. But immediately, in an ironic second thought, he adds «although it would not be the end of the world».

Then he is struck by doubt: perhaps his nephew does not feel able, physically, to take a wife, and he concludes: «...and if you should not feel, of the health of the person to take as wife, it's better to manage to go on living than to kill yourself to make others».

But Leonardo might find himself burdened with a wife who was unhealthy, imperfect or disabled in some way:

«Lionardo... I tell you, that you must not buy a cat in a bag, you must look very closely with your own eyes, because she could be lame or unhealthy...».

But his nephew might misunderstand, and interpret this letter as advice to look for a beautiful wife:

«Lionardo, ... as to beauty, yourself not being the most handsome young man in Florence, you should not give it much importance, as long as she is not actually lame or repulsive...».

Then again the old man raged that his nephew wrote him with little love, telling him he had thrown in the fire a letter that he could not read.

But Leonardo, perhaps because he was far away, more ideal than real, was also the only person to whom Michelangelo spoke of his illnesses, his exhausting work, and his sacrifices.

«Lionardo. ... concerning my illness of being unable to urinate, I have been very sick, day and night without sleep and without rest, and the doctors say that I have the evil of the stone...».

«Lionardo. I wrote you.. of my illness of the stone, which is a most cruel thing, as anyone who has experienced it knows. But having been given to drink a certain water, it made me expel some coarse, white matter in the urine along with some pieces of the stone, so that I am much improved....».

Finally Leonardo decided to marry Cassandra Ridolfi, a relative of Cardinal Niccolò, the son of Contessina.

«Lionardo. In your last letter you tell me you have decided to resume your suit for the woman of the Ridolfi family... this matter has already lasted so long that I'm sick of it, so that I don't know what to write you next... I have waited sixty years thanks to you. Now I am old and I have to think of my family. So take her if you wish. Let what you do be for your own sake and not for me...».

«Lionardo. You have written me that the matter of the daughter of Donato Ridolfi has been settled. For this let God be thanked...».

«Lionardo. I learn from your last letter that you have brought your wife home and you are very satisfied with her, and she sends me her greetings... I want it to be seen that she is the wife of a nephew of mine, but I have not yet been able to do anything about this because Urbino has been away. I've been told that a necklace of valuable pearls would be suitable. I have asked a goldsmith who is a friend of Urbino's to look for one, and I hope to find it. But don't tell her anything yet... Live well and meditate on this, that widows are always far greater in number than widowers...».

«Lionardo. You write me that Cassandra is pregnant. I am very happy to hear this, since I hope that some heir, either male or female, will remain to us... Take care that the name Buonarroto is not lacking in your house, since it has already lasted three hundred years...».

«Lionardo. I learn from your letter that Cassandra has given birth to a fine boy and that she is well, and that you will name him Buonarroto...».

The succession was finally assured, and the imperial blood would continue to flow in the noble veins of the Buonarroti-Simoni di Canossa.

For the good of his soul

ANTONIO DA SANGALLO Junior, the nephew of Giuliano but not a member of the Giamberti family like his famous uncle, had done all he could to curry the favor of Cardinal Farnese. He had worked under the guidance of Bramante, and the future Paul III had commissioned him to restore his palace in Campo de' Fiori. But having become pope, Farnese had requested substantial changes in the project, since the palace of a pope had to be more imposing than that of a cardinal.

When the cornice was to be designed the Pope, unsatisfied with Sangallo's project, turned to other artists and architects living in Rome, among them Perino del Vaga, Fra' Bastiano del Piombo, the young Vasari and Michelangelo.

Michelangelo's drawing was the best, and Sangallo must have been violently resentful when he was asked by the Pope to carry out the project of his rival. He even wrote a detailed memorandum criticizing Michelangelo's solution, invoking in his support the basic principles of Vitruvius.

The Pope did not limit himself to improving his palace. Recalling the plight of his predecessor Clement VII, besieged in Castel Sant'Angelo, he decided to create a belt of fortifications around Rome, and called men of arms and architects to collaborate on this project under the direction of his son Pierluigi Farnese, Duke of Castro.

Michelangelo too was called in, since the Duke knew of the part he had played in the defense of Florence.

«But what do you know about it!, cried Sangallo before the entire commission of experts. «Your art is sculpture and painting, not fortifications!».

«Of painting and sculpture I know little», replied Michelangelo, «but of fortifying, with the experience I have had, I know more than you and all those of your family».

Soon he presented the Pope with a complete project for fortifying Borgo, and, as if on purpose, Sangallo was commissioned to implement it.

When Sangallo died in 1546 Paul III issued a brief appointing Michelangelo chief architect, «Commisarius, Praefectus et Operarius», of the Fabric of Saint Peter's.

«Paul III was inspired by God», states Vasari.

Michelangelo accepted, with a heavy heart, setting two conditions: that he be given full power to act as he wished, and that he be paid no recompense, having taken on that heavy burden only for the good of his soul.

For the good of his soul Michelangelo had painted at the head of the stairs, in his house in Macel de' Corvi, a skeleton carrying under its arm a coffin. Under it these verses could be read:

> *I say to you, that to the world have given*
> *Soul and body and spirit all together:*
> *In this dark case is your true place.*

Obviously, lighthearted joy did not reign in that house. Even the name of the area, *il Macello de' Corvi* or Raven's Place, has a sinister sound to it. It conjures up the image of a dark, dismal house with windows almost always closed and door locked tight, exactly the opposite of what an artist's home should be and must have been at the time.

And the house really was like that; near the ruins Trajan's Forum (where the Tomb of the Unknown Soldier stands today), narrow and cramped, composed of five rooms, a loggia, a ground floor and an orchard.

In a mood of black humor the illustrious inhabitant of the house described to his friend Francesco Berni the filthy squalor around it, where the alleys reeked with urine worse than a latrine.

But the artist stayed where he was. Even after he became rich he never thought of leaving that hovel to live in a palace. He stayed there over thirty years, from the day of his arrival in Rome until his death.

Michelangelo slept in an iron bed with a straw mattress. In a corner of his bedroom was a «big cupboard made of boards» in which he kept his clothes and linen. In another corner was a «big walnut chest locked with a key» where he kept his drawings and money.

Probably there was a wooden chair as well; certainly there were plenty of cobwebs.

The faithful Francesco Armadori, nicknamed Urbino, was his servant for over twenty-five years. Much more than a servant, Urbino was by turns a devoted pupil, the manager of the house and workshop, nurse and cashier, servant and secretary.

«What will you do, Urbino, if I die?»

«Unfortunately, I will have to serve another».

«Poor Urbino!», replied Michelangelo. «But I want to shelter you in your misfortune, I want to make you rich!». And he made him a gift of two thousand *scudi*, a fabulous sum. He allowed Urbino not only to marry, but to bring into the home his young wife along with a maid who served them all. Lastly, he was godfather to Urbino's first son, whom they named Michelangelo.

When Urbino fell severely ill, Michelangelo asked his nephew Leonardo to request some devoted person to watch over the bedside of his faithful companion, never leaving him alone.

«Your know how Urbino died», he wrote later to Vasari, «to the infinite grace of God, but to my great loss and boundless grief. The grace was that where in life he helped me to live, in dying he has taught me to die, not with displeasure, but with a desire for death. I kept him twenty-six years and found him most true and faithful. And now that I have made him rich and thought he would be the staff to lean on in my old age, he is gone; nor have I any hope but to see him again in Paradise. And of this God sent me a sign in the most happy death he gave him. Much more than at the thought of dying I am grieved at being left alive in this treacherous world with all its cares; although the better part of me has gone already, there being left to me only infinite misery».

Not even for the death of Vittoria Colonna had Michelangelo's grief been expressed in such ardent terms; and time did not fade the memory of that affectionate companionship. He remained in close contact the widow, listening to her like a father and consoling her as well as he could.

One by one his friends were departing before him, leaving him older and lonelier. The chisel and the brush weighed heavily, by now, in his tired hands. Now painting and sculpture gave way to prayers.

The fourth muse

S culpture, painting, architecture – three arts, three muses. Poetry was for Michelangelo «the fourth muse», but also the most controversial one.

Undoubtedly he began by imitating and not through sudden inspiration, as is normally the case with poets. He set himself to writing verses because everyone was doing it. It was the fashion of the times. He knew how to compose a sonnet because it was almost obligatory for anyone who lived in a moderately cultured environment. Even Savonarola wrote poetry. The learned conversations of the humanists, the poetic vein of the Magnificent, Poliziano's *stanze*, served as daily stimulus to the artist. In the palace on Via Larga poetry was like a contagious disease. The official poets, after Poliziano, were Bembo, Tebaldeo, Aquilano, Molza; Boiardo and Ariosto; Vittoria Colonna and the comical Berni. As for himself, Michelangelo never claimed to be a poet.

It was a contemporary of his, Benedetto Varchi, who led the way to applause with a comment on one of Michelangelo's sonnets that has become famous.

«The sonnet certainly comes from me, but the comment comes from heaven... I feel, for his words and praise, to be that which I am not...» wrote the artist to a friend. Nor could he say otherwise, as an honest man who approached poetry with humility, aware that it was not «his art».

But now admiration had silenced the critics, and Michelangelo could write nothing that was not immediately praised to the stars. If he composed a sonnet his friends copied it and passed it from hand to hand, from city to city. If it were a madrigal it was put to music and sung even by boys in the street. Comparing Michelangelo to Dante became a commonplace. But to which Dante? To the poet of the rhymes, harsh and bitter in language, so different from the *Vita Nova* of his youth and the *Divine Comedy* of his maturity.

Like all of the poets of his age Michelangelo imitated Petrarca. But he was not gifted with the facile vein of his contemporaries, and was not satisfied with similes drawn from traditional sources. He attempted, with obvious effort, to imbue his poetry with thought, his own thought. To do this he drew paragons and images from his sculptor's art, and it is this that makes his poetry so individual, so different from that of all other poets.

Michelangelo's poetry, like his painting, has no landscapes, but always and only a thought on which the entire poetic discourse hinges. When this thought had been fully expressed, even in a few lines, he felt the composition to be finished, although it might form an imperfect sonnet.

His themes were love and death, good and guilt, man and God. From pallid literary love he gradually went on to pagan love for Tommaso Cavalieri and Christian love for Vittoria Colonna. From the irony of the days when he was frescoing the vault of the Sistine Chapel he went on to the grieving pessimism of the last of his *Pietà*; from the contemplation of life to the contemplation of death.

> *I have seen some of his compositions;*
> *I am ignorant; and yet I would say I had*
> *Read them all in Plato*

declared Berni. And Condivi added: «...that he not only has loved human beauty, but universally everything beautiful, a beautiful horse, a beautiful dog, a beautiful fish, a beautiful plant, a beautiful mountain, a beautiful forest..., admiring them with marvelous affection».

His poems were to meet an unhappy fate. They were supposed to be published while he was still alive. He himself had selected and transcribed most of them in a notebook. They were instead published, under the title of *Rhymes*, only in 1623 by one of his great-nephews. But Michelangelo the Younger did not want to publish the poems as they were. Those written for Tommaso de' Cavalieri, for example, could have cast a shadow of suspicion on his illustrious ancestor. With good intentions he set himself to revising them, eliminating the obscure parts, smoothing and softening «with one eye on the Holy Office and the other on the theologians in Santa Croce». Here is an example:

> *If vanquished and captured I must be blessed,*
> *No marvel is it if, naked and alone*
> *I remain the prisoner of a Cavalier in arms*

The open allusion to the handsome Tommaso de' Cavalieri was upsetting to the artist's prudish great-nephew, who revised the poem as follows:

> *If therefore amid torments I am blessed,*
> *No marvel is it if, helpless and alone,*
> *I yearn toward a heart with virtue armed*

«because the ignorance of men has field to murmur». And so for almost two centuries, poems that were not those of Michelangelo were commented. Even Foscolo was the victim of this error, although in his critical essay on Michelangelo he tried with passionate attention to penetrate into the soul of the artist.

The real *Rhymes* were published only in 1863, in Florence, by Cesare Guasti, opening the way at last to new and more reliable research.

To return from history to criticism, Michelangelo's last compositions should be viewed separately from the rest of his poetry. He was always a firm believer in the power of prayer. In his deep religious convictions he felt he had to pray and thank God when fortune seemed to abandon him, in times of failure and defeat. Many of his letters bear witness to this heroic humility that made his spirit that of a giant.

But the prayer of his last years, written in grief-filled hendecasyllables, worked miracles. It freed him at last from any literary model, letting him speak in a language that is unmistakably his alone. It sublimated his concepts into the highest images, expressed in true, pure, absolute poetry. It truly brought him to speak with God, put him in contact with the absolute, granting him at last the grace of hope.

One of these poems alone is enough to demonstrate the dignity that places Michelangelo's poetry on the same level as his greatest works in the other three arts:

> *Already has my life reached its end*
> *The fragile bark through stormy seas enters*
> *That common harbor where, arriving*
> > *We must account for every good or evil work*
> *Where loving fantasy*
> *of which art was for me idol and monarch,*
> *Was, I now know well, with error laden*
> > *And what each man, despite himself, desires.*
> *Loving thoughts, once vain and glad,*
> *What are they now, when two deaths approach?*
> > *Certain I am of one, the other threatens me.*
> *Nor painting nor sculpture can do more than calm*
> *The soul, yearning toward that divine love*
> > *Opening its arms to take us on the cross.*

In slow, solemn rhythm the lyrical motif develops and expands, calling back the soul from its wanderings. Art, idol and monarch, is recognized and unveiled. All of his giants made of stone, the multitude of painted figures, seem to bow down with him in meditation. Painting and sculpture are no longer enough, offer no response to the soul anxiously seeking another reality. And a Christ who is more than an immense, cosmic presence is sculpted in the last verse in a gesture that goes beyond any figurative image.

The enthusiasm of Tiberio

A YOUNG MAN CALLED Tiberio Calcagni had been brought to the house in Macel de' Corvi by the Florentine exiles, recommended in particular by the banker Francesco Bandini. He was a bright intelligent boy, soon welcomed as a friend by Michelangelo. The old misanthrope could be quickly moved to feeling when he met with respect, sincerity, sympathy, intelligence and humility.

Patiently Michelangelo began to supervise the work of his young fellow citizen, encouraging him, inspiring him with confidence, although he was still a beginner. After a year of diligent study Tiberio had gained the master's trust and affection. That trust was well placed, since it was never to be deceived.

«Antonio», Calcagni asked Michelangelo's servant one day, «what are those broken pieces of marble under the loggia?»

«That is a Deposition, Messer Tiberio».

«A Deposition? By Michelangelo?»

«Now it is mine, Messer Tiberio. The master gave it to me many years ago, when I was still the assistant of poor Urbino».

«What are you saying, Antonio? Tell me, I must know the story».

Antonio related that, since 1545, between one work and another, while engaged in painting the Pauline Chapel, Michelangelo had begun to rough out a Deposition from an ancient piece of marble that must have been an enormous capital on one of the columns in Vespasian's temple of peace.

«He had to work with the heavy chisel, if you know what I mean. If he stopped working his health suffered for it. The more he worked, the better he felt. But that marble was extremely hard, and full of veins. Michelangelo was old, but he made the chips fly faster than three young boys put together. You can't imagine how the sparks were flying!».

«And then?»

«Then one day, in the fury of polishing it, he gave the Madonna's elbow a blow that broke off too much marble. At least he thought it was too much, although you couldn't really see it. It was a beautiful group, with the dead Christ supported by his Mother, assisted by Nicodemus and the Magdalene: four figures, in full relief, with a hooded Nicodemus whose good, sad face looks so much like that of our own Messer Michelangelo.

«We will give it to some church, perhaps Santa Maria Maggiore», he often said, «and we will make sure that it serves for my tomb as well».

Tiberio was impatient to hear the end of the story.

«But that blow on the elbow so enraged him», continued Antonio, «that in his anger he took the hammer and began to strike it like a madman, saying that it had turned out bad because that pest Urbino was always under his feet annoying him. So I found the courage to ask him not to destroy that group, to be content with having spoiled it, and to give it to me. And now it is mine».

«And now», exclaimed Tiberio, «since you can do nothing with a broken statue, give it to me. I will restore it and I'll give you something in exchange».

Michelangelo, informed of their agreement, smilingly consented. Tiberio brought the pieces to a vineyard owned by his protector Francesco Bandi, near Monte Cavallo, where Daniele da Volterra also worked, and patiently began to reassemble the group.

Once in a while Michelangelo went to watch them working on that Deposition, giving them suggestions and finally approving the restoration. Although the work differs from the original drawing, especially in the Magdalene sculpted by Calcagni, it is still a masterpiece. The dead Christ, his body drooping despite the support of his Mother and Nicodemus, is the image of physical annihilation, in counterpoise to the living anguish of those who uphold him. Nicodemus, severe and austere, resembles the hooded figure with folded arms in the Crucifixion of Peter in the Pauline Chapel, that other grieving self-portrait.

Bramante's heritage

PAUL III, WHO died in 1549, was succeeded by Cardinal Del Monte, who took the name of Julius III. «Here we are awaiting the new Pope from hour to hour. God knows how the Christians need him and enough», Michelangelo had written his nephew a few weeks earlier. But the new Pope wanted only to enjoy his throne in peace. Having been one of the most important intermediaries in bringing about the final agreements with the heirs of Julius II, he knew Michelangelo and showed him favor at once by siding with him against the Wardens of the Fabric of Saint Peter's.

To understand this dispute we must go back to its origin, to the time when Julius II, to make place for his tomb, had commissioned Bramante to rebuild the Basilica.

Bramante, having drawn up a project, began the work of demolition assisted by Raphael, by Fra' Giocondo da Verona and by Giuliano da Sangallo, later bequeathing his project and the management of the Fabric to Raphael. At Raphael's death his assistants, Baldassarre Peruzzi and Antonio da Sangallo Junior went on with the work under the reign of Pope Clement VII. But war and the sack of Rome tightened the papal purse-strings and the work was suspended. When it was resumed, under Paul III, Antonio da Sangallo was made director, a post he held until his death.

Michelangelo, having been granted full powers by the Pope, realized that Bramante's original project had been not merely changed, but actually transformed by his successors. Accordingly, he decided to make a new model that would more faithfully reflect Bramante's conception.

Sangallo however had surrounded himself with supporters, persons who «drew from that work, more than honor, gain», all agreed to prevent the implementation of Bramante's project through any means, including slander and sabotage.

The rumors reached Florence, and a friend of Michelangelo's, Giovan Francesco Ughi, wrote to warn him: «...In the past I have not written you, as I had no occasion to do so; nor would I have written you now, but that Jacopo del Conte has come here with the wife of Nanni di Baccio Bigio, who says he has beaten her, because Nanni has so much work to do for Saint Peter's. Among other things she says that he is making a model for that work that will be better than your drawing. Take care, because she says you are doing crazy, childish things; and that he is determined to have you thrown down; that he is favored by the Pope as much as you; that you squander an infinite amount of money, and that you work by night so you cannot be seen...».

Michelangelo sent the letter to one of the Wardens of the Fabric who was his friend, writing on it: «Messer Bartolommeo, please read this letter, and consider who are these two rogues that... lie like this in the information they give the Wardens».

But the Wardens had little sympathy for Michelangelo, since the full powers granted him by the Pope deprived them of power. They sent the Pope a report in Latin listing all of the expenses authorized by the artist and emphasizing that *de ipso autem aedificio, quale futurum sit, Deputati nullam possunt reddere rationem, quibus omnibus occultantur tamquam extraneis*, that is, they could express no opinion on the current or future state of the Basilica because they were kept as uninformed as if they had nothing to do with it.

Starting in the time of Paul III the accusations of the «Sangallo sect», backed up by the complaints of the Wardens, continued under Julius III, causing the latter to summon them all before him along with Michelangelo.

The Pope addressed the sculptor: «These Wardens maintain that the King's niche, where there are three chapels with three windows above them, has little light».

«I wish to hear these Wardens speak as well», answered Michelangelo.

«Here we are», arrogantly replied Cardinal Cervini.

«Monsignor», the artist explained, «above those windows will be another three in the vault».

«But you never told us that», protested the Cardinal.

«I am not, nor do I wish to be, obliged to say, either to your Excellency or to anyone else, what I must and will do!», exploded Michelangelo. «Your duty is that of collecting money and protecting it against thieves, and the project of the Fabric you will leave to me. Holy Father», he added turning to the Pope, «you see what I gain from this. If this hard labor that I endure does not do my soul good, I am only wasting time and work».

Julius III clapped a friendly hand on his shoulder:

«Michelangelo, you are gaining much for your soul and for your body too, have no doubt of it».

And before the Wardens, silent and resentful, he reconfirmed Michelangelo's appointment as supreme architect «with all authority and responsibility to do and undo according to his judgement, to hire and fire workers, to operate according to the money he has been given, but in expenses to consider, rather than economy, the magnificence of the work and the greatness of its design».

Why had such great changes been made in Bramante's project? Modern critics say that there was an organic flaw in it, the supports being too fragile for the enormous mass of the vault. First Raphael, then Sangallo, in the attempt to reinforce them, had changed the proportions of the building. The church had been lengthened to form a Latin cross, and the cupola was sustained by real buttresses.

In spite of their years of enmity Michelangelo was serenely honest in recognizing Bramante's merits, stating that all those who had «deviated» from his project – such as Sangallo – had abandoned the true way.

«Yet Sangallo's model still offers good pasture», an assistant objected one day.

«Yes, for animals, and oxen like yourself who know nothing of architecture», replied Michelangelo.

To leave an irrefutable document, he found two master carpenters and called them to Macel de' Corvi to make a wooden model of the new Basilica.

When this was done he had another made in terracotta, and then a final, larger wooden model that was finished only in 1561.

Michelangelo's dome was completely spherical in shape, but the last architects, twenty-five years later, raised the keystone of the vault five meters to lessen the lateral thrust and give more space to perspective.

Homesick for Florence

IN THE LONG tragedy of the Fabric of Saint Peter's, the final tragedy of the aging Michelangelo was to intermingle and conclude. Cosimo de' Medici, first Duke, then Grand Duke of Florence, had sent to call for him, wanting him back in his own city again. Although some biographers have stated that Michelangelo refused to return in the name of republican freedom, this is not true. The artist wanted to return to his city, hoped to do so, and openly said so. He asked Cosimo's messengers only for enough time to leave the Fabric of Saint Peter's at a point where it could no longer be changed, after which he would return to Florence to live out his last days in peace.

To Urbino's widow too he confirmed his intention of returning to his own city, telling her not to send little Michelangelo, his godson, to Rome «because I am without women and without governing, and the child is too tender». As soon as he had left the Fabric in good state and arranged his affairs, however, «I think... this Winter I will go to Florence for good, because I am old, and I have no time to return again to Rome. I will visit you; and if you wish to give me Michelagniolo I will keep him in Florence with more love than the sons of Leonardo my nephew, teaching him what I know, that his father wanted him to learn».

Julius III had died by now. One day he had told Michelangelo he wanted to have him embalmed to keep him with him and make him as eternal as his works. The Pope was the first to go instead, dying in 1555.

Cardinal Cervini was elected Pope under the name of Marcellus II, and Michelangelo, remembering their quarrel when the cardinal had been one of the Wardens of the Fabric of Saint Peter's, thought of fleeing Rome.

The new Pope, however, reigned only 22 days, and was succeeded by Cardinal Carafa, who took the name of Paul IV.

This Pope too was no friend to Michelangelo. On the very day of his coronation he abolished the stipend of 1200 gold *scudi* a year, coming from the tolls collected in the Port of Piacenza, which had been assigned the artist by the Farnese Pope, and even considered having the *Last Judgement* scraped off the walls of the Sistine Chapel. But Paul IV was to die after four years as Pope. After a four-month-long conclave, on Christmas morning of 1550, Cardinal Angelo de' Medici from Milan was elected Pope under the name of Pius IV. He was not related to Cosimo, and to distinguish him from the Florentine family he was called *medichino*.

While still a cardinal he had frequently claimed to be a relative of the Duke of Florence, just as Cosimo, now that the *medichino* had been made pope, pretended the same thing.

The new Pope proposed «to reduce the heretics to obedience and the priests to the canons», but did not neglect Michelangelo, for whom he felt sincere affection, and who just at that time was being subjected to the worst insults from the followers of Sangallo, Nanni di Baccio Bigio in particular. Despite his ignorance of architecture Nanni had offered to take Michelangelo's place as director of the Fabric of Saint Peter's. Through intrigue he managed to have himself appointed «first assistant» to Michelangelo, after Cesare da Castel Durante, the sculptor's aid, had been mysteriously murdered. Michelangelo, who visited the Fabric only rarely due to his age, found out that Nanni had entered Saint Peter's as master, ordering this to be done, that to be undone, at great risk to the building.

In a burst of new-found energy Michelangelo went to meet the Pope in Piazza del Campidoglio. He was too enraged to speak. The Pope had him enter a room, calmed him, and asked him to explain clearly what he wanted.

«Holiness», gasped the old artist shaking with indignation, «the Wardens have put as my replacement one that I do no know. If they and Your Holiness wish me to be involved no longer I will return to Florence, where I will be welcomed by that good duke who has so much desired me, and I will end my life in my own home; but I ask your permission».

The Pope, concerned, asked him to wait a few days, saying that he would call him again after having heard what the Wardens had to say.

He then convened the Wardens to find out what was happening. They confirmed to him that the Fabric was full of mistakes and threatening to collapse.

But the Pope did not trust this report, and charged Gabrio Serbelloni, a trusted relative of his, to make a thorough inspection of the Basilica.

It was found that the work on the Fabric was going well and that the Wardens, in bad faith, had given credit to the slander and lies of Nanni di Baccio Bigio.

«Throw him out!», ordered the Pope.

Michelangelo's enemy «was chased away», writes Vasari, «with words of little decency, from that Fabric, in the presence of many gentlemen».

Through a subsequent *motu proprio* Pius IV not only reconfirmed Michelangelo's full powers over the Fabric but also gave strict instructions that no changes be made in his project, either now or in the future. Once again the old fighter, though isolated by fatigue and his lofty position, had triumphed.

The tallow candle

O NE DAY VASARI wrote Michelangelo from Florence to inform him that the eldest son of Cosimo, Francesco de' Medici, had left for Rome and «knowing how much the duke his father loves and honors you» wanted to meet him.

The old artist obediently went to pay homage.

The young prince greeted him, rising to his feet and holding his hat in his hand as a sign of respect. Michelangelo, always sensitive to such gestures, was moved, and wrote Vasari that he was sorry to be old because he would have liked to make something for Don Francesco. Being unable to do anything else, «I will look for some beautiful antique to send him in Florence».

From much further away, from France where she had become queen, another descendent of the Medici, Catherine, wrote to ask him for an equestrian monument in memory of her husband Henry II.

Michelangelo was unable to say no. He agreed with the queen that he would make the model and Daniele da Volterra would sculpt the statue.

As if having foreseen his imminent death, everyone was asking him for something, and he replied to all of them.

Vasari reminded him of an old project for the Library of San Lorenzo. Searching in his memory, Michelangelo apologized: «A certain staircase comes back clearly to me, but I don't think it is the one I designed then, because it seems clumsy; however, I will write it here», and he drew it, adding a detailed description. Not content, he made a clay model and sent it «arranged in a box», to Bartolommeo Ammannati.

At the request of Cosimo he made five drawings for a church of the Florentines in Rome. He supervised the work on the Campidoglio conducted by Tommaso de' Cavalieri, and designed for Pius IV the tomb of his brother the Marquis of Marignano as well as Porta Pia and the Church of Santa Maria degli Angeli.

The bale of merchandise

IT WAS FEBRUARY. A stiff cold wind was blowing, bringing sudden heavy showers of rain. That morning Antonio had not saddled the horse, hoping that Michelangelo would stay at home in such weather.

But the old man was already descending the stairs wrapped in his warm mantle of fox fur.

«Quick, Antonio. What have you been doing up to now?»

«Messer Michelangelo, it's no weather to be out in today. It's cold and it's raining. And then last night I heard you hammering, you must be tired».

«Let me go, Antonio. What can I do if I find no peace anywhere?».

At that moment his disciple Tiberio Calcagni arrived.

«Oh Messer Michelangelo, you are still here, good».

«What is it?»

«You shouldn't go out today, in this weather, with this rain».

«Tiberio, what can I do? I am restless and can find peace nowhere».

With these words, assisted by the faithful Antonio, Michelangelo mounted his horse and started off for Saint Peter's.

Some days later Diomede Leoni, now like Calcagni a frequent visitor to Macel de' Corvi who tried to help the old master when he could, wrote to Leonardo Buonarroti in Florence «to inform you of the condition of Messer up to this hour, which is the third hour of the night. I left him a little while ago out of bed, having good understanding and awareness but plagued by a continuous somnolence, of which to cure himself, between the hours of twenty-two and twenty-three, he wanted to go out riding, as he used to do every evening when the weather was good...».

Michelangelo refused to give up. He tried to «mock» the death that was assaulting him with its first drowsiness by riding out – in February! – to get some fresh air.

«When he fell ill», writes Daniele da Volterra to Vasari, «which was a Monday in Carnival time, he sent for me, as he always did... When he saw me he said: Oh, Daniello, I am done for, but I beg of you, don't abandon me. And he had me write a letter to Messer Lionardo his nephew, that he should come, and to me he said that I should wait there in the house and never leave. And this I did, although I felt more ill than well. His illness lasted five days, two sitting by the fire and three in bed. So that he expired on Friday evening, in peace as we may surely believe...».

It was February 18, 1564.

«I leave my soul in the hands of God», he said with a feeble but unwavering voice, «my body to the earth, and my belongings to my relatives. My friends», he added in a whisper, «now recall to me the sufferings of Jesus».

When Leonardo arrived the body had already been taken to the Church of the Santi Apostoli, and the Governor of Rome had already made an inventory of the house in the presence of Daniele and Tommaso de' Cavalieri.

In the room «where he was used to sleep» they found:
«– an iron bed with a straw pallet
– three mattresses
– two woolen blankets and one of white sheepskin
– a fox-fur mantle
– a long coat-dress
– a locked box containing seven to eight thousand *scudi*, many drawings and a cartoon in several pieces showing the plan of the Fabric of Saint Peter's».

«In a room below, roofed over» (that is, in the studio):
«– a statue begun for a Saint Peter, roughed-out but not finished
– another statue begun for a Christ and another figure above, attached together and not finished (that is, the Rondanini Pietà)
– another small statue for a Christ bearing the cross on his shoulders, unfinished».

In the loggia on the ground floor:
« – the forge, with two small bellows
– a barrel to keep fodder
– some large sticks of firewood».

In the stall «a little chestnut nag, with saddle and bridle».

His nephew Leonardo, «immediately ordered that the body be brought to Florence, as he had commanded us many times when he was well, and also two days before his death», wrote Daniele da Volterra to Vasari.

But the nephew, having been informed that the Pope was actually offering the Basilica of Saint Peter's as burial place for Michelangelo and afraid to disappoint Cosimo de' Medici, had the bad idea of arranging with the Florentine ambassador for the body to be taken away secretly.

After the solemn funeral in the Church of the Santi Apostoli, the coffin was concealed in a bale of wool and loaded onto a freight cart.

On March 11th the body of the «divine» Michelangelo was unloaded, along with the bales of merchandise, at the customs house in Florence; and by night, like smuggled goods, it was brought into the city.

Life of Michelangelo - Events in history and art

1475 On March 6th Michelangelo is born at Caprese, near Arezzo, the second child of the Magistrate Ludovico Buonarroti and of Francesca, daughter of Neri di Miniato del Serra and Bonda Rucellai. The family soon moves to Florence and Michelangelo is put out to nurse in nearby Settignano.

1478 In Florence the Pazzi conspiracy against the Medici fails.

1482 At about this time Sandro Botticelli paints the Birth of Venus and the Allegory of Spring.

1483 Raphael is born in Urbino.

1487 Michelangelo enters the workshop of Domenico Ghirlandaio in Florence but leaves it sooner than expected. Two years later he begins to frequent the garden of the Monastery of San Marco with its sculptures from the Medicean collections.

1492 Around this date Michelangelo sculpts a Crucifix for the Florentine church of Santo Spirito as well as the *Battle of the Centaurs* and the *Madonna of the Stairs*. Lorenzo the Magnificent dies.

1494 The artist leaves Florence, going first to Venice and then to Bologna, where he sculpts three statues for the tomb of San

Domenico. Charles VIII, King of France, leads his army against Florence, encountering no resistance. After his departure, Piero de' Medici is exiled and a republican government set up under the influence of Fra Girolamo Savonarola.

1495 Returns to Florence where he sculpts a *Saint John the Baptist* and a *Sleeping Cupid*, both lost to posterity.

1496 Settles in Rome, where he begins the statue of *Bacchus*. Alexander VI Borgia is elected Pope.

1498 On August 27 Michelangelo signs a contract with the French Cardinal Jean Bilhères for the *Pietà*. He promises to finish the work within a year, for a price of four-hundred-fifty ducats. In Florence Savonarola is condemned to be burned at the stake.

1499 Finishes the *Pietà* in Saint Peter's Basilica.

1501 Returns to Florence. Signs a contract for fifteen statues for the Piccolomini altar in the Duomo of Siena. He is commissioned to sculpt the *David*. In Florence, Piero Soderini is elected Gonfalonier (title equivalent to that of Doge in Venice).

1503 Signs a contract to sculpt twelve statues of apostles to be placed in the Florence Duomo. The contract will be cancelled later and the only statue to be completed will be the *Saint Matthew*. Around this time he executes the *Taddei Tondo* and the *Pitti Tondo*. Alexander VI dies. Pius VI Piccolomini is elected Pope but dies only ten days later, succeeded by Julius II Della Rovere.

1504 The *David* is placed in Piazza della Signoria. Michelangelo finishes the *Bruges Madonna and Child*, the *Saint Matthew* and the cartoon (now lost) for the *Battle of Cascina*.

1505 He is called to Rome by Pope Julius II and commissioned to build the Pope's tomb, originally destined to Saint Peter's Basilica but later constructed in San Pietro in Vincoli.

1506 Flees back to Florence after quarreling with Pope Julius II over the work on the tomb. Piero Soderini convinces him to meet the Pope in Bologna, where they are reconciled. In 1506-1507 he completes the *Doni Tondo*. Bramante begins working on the new Basilica of Saint Peter's in Vatican. Julius II conquers Perugia and is given the keys to the city of Urbino. Giovanni II Bentivoglio, lord of Bologna, abandons the city and the Pope makes a triumphal entry.

1508 Finishes a colossal statue, a portrait in bronze of Julius II, which is placed above the portal of San Petronio (now lost). Returns to Rome and begins frescoing the ceiling of the Sistine Chapel. Raphael begins to fresco the rooms of Julius II's apartment in the Vatican Palace.

1509 The League of Cambrai, led by Julius II, defeats Venice at Agnadello.

1512 Finishes frescoing the ceiling of the Sistine Chapel twenty days before its reopening on October 31. In Florence Soderini's government is overthrown and the Medici return to power.

1513 After the death of Julius II, stipulates with his heirs a new contract for his tomb; sculpts the *Moses* and the two *Slaves* now in the Louvre. Leo X de' Medici is elected Pope.

1514 Signs a contract for the *Christ Bearing the Cross* in the Church of Santa Maria sopra Minerva in Rome. Bramante dies; Raphael succeeds him as architect of the Fabric of Saint Peter's and begins decorating the Stanze with the *Fire in the Borgo*.

1516 Charles of Hapsburg, the future Charles V, is King of Spain.

1516 Moves back to Florence to work on the project of the façade of San Lorenzo.

1517 The Protestant Reformation movement begins in Germany.

Francesco della Rovere takes back the Duchy of Urbino which had been given to the Pope's nephew, Lorenzo de' Medici.

1519 Begins the *Captives*. Charles V is crowned Emperor. Leonardo da Vinci dies at Amboise. Pontormo begins frescoing the Medicean villa of Poggio a Caiano.

1520 Is released from any commitment as regards the façade of San Lorenzo. Begins work on the New Sacristy in the same church. Giulio Romano paints the *Battle of Ponte Milvio* in the Constantine Room in the Vatican. Raphael paints the *Transfiguration*; dies at Rome the same year.

1522 Hadrian VI of Utrecht is elected Pope.

1523 Francesco Maria della Rovere resumes negotiations for the tomb of Julius II. Michelangelo continues to work on the New Sacristy in San Lorenzo. Hadrian VI dies and is succeeded by Clement VII de' Medici.

1524 Begins work on the Laurentian Library in Florence.

1525 Battle of Pavia. The King of France Francis I, an ally of the Pope, is defeated and taken prisoner by the army of Emperor Charles V. In Florence Pontormo begins the frescos in Santa Felicita.

1526 League of Cognac: Florence, France, the Papacy, Venice and Milan join forces against Charles V.

1527 Work on the New Sacristy is interrupted when the Medici are driven out of Florence. Rome is sacked by the Lanzichenecchi of the Imperial troops. Many artists flee the city.

1529 Michelangelo is appointed director of the work of fortifying Florence, besieged by the Imperialist army. On September 21 he flees to Venice, fearing for his life. He paints a *Leda* for the

Duke of Ferrara. Charles V concludes the Pact of Barcelona with the Pope. He is promised the Imperial crown in exchange for his aid in reinstating the Medici at Florence.

1530 Sculpts an *Apollo* for Baccio Valori. Resumes work on the New Sacristy. The Imperial army conquers Florence. Charles V is crowned Emperor by Clement VII at Bologna.

1531 Return of Alessandro de' Medici to Florence after the brief interval of republican government.

1532 New contract for the tomb of Julius II.

1534 Finishes the *Victory*. Leaves Florence definitively for Rome. Clement VII dies, succeeded by Paul III Farnese. Ignazio di Loyola founds the Company of Jesus.

1536 Michelangelo begins to fresco the *Last Judgement* on the end wall of the Sistine Chapel in the Vatican Palace. Calvinist reformation at Geneva.

1540 Finishes the bust of *Brutus* begun the year before.

1541 Completes the *Last Judgement*.

1545 The statues are placed on the tomb of Julius II in San Pietro in Vincoli in Rome. The Council of Trent is convened; the Catholic Counter-Reformation is launched.

1546 Antonio da Sangallo the Younger dies. Michelangelo replaces Antonio as Vatican architect; begins designing the dome of Saint Peter's.

1547 Begins the *Pietà Rondanini*.

1547 Vittoria Colonna, friend and correspondent of Michelangelo, dies.

1550 Begins the *Pietà Bandini*.

1564 Michelangelo dies on February 18th at his home in Rome, leaving the *Pietà Rondanini* unfinished. Daniele da Volterra is commissioned to paint over the parts of the *Last Judgement* deemed obscene.

Michelangelo's works - Topographical index

Baden (Zurich)
Private collection
Madonna and Child (of uncertain attribution, 1510?)

Basel
Private collection
Saint John the Evangelist (1490-1492?)

Bologna
Basilica di San Domenico
Kneeling Angel (1494-1495)
Saint Petronius (1494-1495)
Saint Proculus (1494-1495)

Bruges
Onze Lieve Vrouwkerk (Notre-Dame)
Madonna and Child (1498-1501)

Dublin
National Gallery of Ireland
Holy Family with the Infant Saint John the Baptist (1490?)

Florence
Accademia Gallery
David (1501-1504)

Saint Matthew (1503-1504)
Pietà from Palestrina (of uncertain attribution, c. 1550)
Young Captive (1530-1534)
Bearded Captive (1530-1534)
Captive "Atlas" (1530-1534)
Awakening Captive (1530-1534)

Palazzo Vecchio
Battle of Cascina (1505-1506)
Victory (1532-1534 circa)

Casa Buonarroti
Battle of the Centaurs (1491-1492)
Wooden model for the façade of San Lorenzo (1519 circa)
Madonna of the Stairs (1490-1492)
Crucifix (1492-1493)
River God (1524 circa)
Hercules-Samson (1525 circa)

Museo dell'Opera del Duomo
Bandini Pietà (1550-1555)

Bargello National Museum
David-Apollo (1525-1530)
Madonna and Child with the Infant Saint John
  (or *Pitti Tondo*) (1503-1506)
Bacchus (1496-1497)
Brutus (1538 circa)

San Lorenzo
Madonna and Child (or *Medici Madonna*) (1521-1534)
Sarcophagus of Lorenzo de' Medici
  (*Lorenzo de' Medici* 1525 circa; *Dawn*, 1524-1527;
  Dusk, 1524-1531)
Sarcophagus of Giuliano de' Medici
  (*Giuliano de' Medici* 1526-1534; *Day*, 1526-1531;
  Night, 1526-1531)

Santa Maria Novella, Cappella Maggiore
Dormitio Virginis (1488-1490)
Baptism of Christ (1488-1490)

The Uffizi
Holy Family with the Infant Saint John the Baptist
  (or *Doni Tondo*) (1506-1507)

Florence - Architecture
Façade of San Lorenzo (designed in 1518, never built)
New Sacristy of San Lorenzo (begun in 1521)
Laurentian Library (1524-1560)

London
National Gallery
Madonna and Child with the Infant Saint John and Four Angels
  (or *Manchester Madonna*) (1510?)
Deposition in the Tomb (1511?)

Royal Academy
Madonna and Child with the Infant Saint John
  (or *Taddei Madonna*; or *Taddei Tondo*) (1503 circa)

Milan
Castello Sforzesco
Rondanini Pietà (after 1552)

New York
Private collection
Madonna and Child with the Infant Saint John (1510*)

Padova
Choir of the Cathedral (1552-1570)

Paris
Louvre
Dying Slave (or *Sleeping Slave*) (1513)
Rebellious Slave (1513)

Rome
Sistine Chapel
Frescoed ceiling (1508-1512)
Last Judgement (1537-1541)

Saint Peter's in Vatican
Pietà (1497-1498)

Vatican Palace, Pauline Chapel
Conversion of Saint Paul (1542-1545)
Crucifixion of Saint Peter (1545-1560)

San Pietro in Vincoli
Tomb of Julius II (completed in 1545) including:
  Moses (1515 circa)

Santa Maria sopra Minerva
Christ Bearing the Cross (1518-1520)

Rome - Architecture
Stairway of Palazzo Senatorio (1540 circa)
Santa Maria Maggiore, Sforza Chapel (1559)
Porta Pia (1561)
Capitoline Hill (designed 1538 or 1546)
Castel Sant'Angelo - Chapel of Leo X (1514)
Saint Peter's in Vatican (started 1546)

Siena
Duomo
Saint Paul (1503-1504)
Saint Peter (1503-1504)
Saint Pius (1503-1504)
Saint Gregory (1503-1504)

Vienna
Akademie der bildenden Künste
Madonna and Child with the Infant Saint John (1495?)

Index